ONE IMMIGRANT
in a WORLD of MANY

AN AMERICAN STORY OF SURVIVAL

Andrea Bermúdez

ARCHWAY
PUBLISHING

Archway Publishing books may be ordered through booksellers or by contacting:

Archway Publishing
1663 Liberty Drive
Bloomington, IN 47403
www.archwaypublishing.com
1 (888) 242-5904

Interior Image Credit: Andrea Bermúdez

ISBN: 978-1-4808-9049-7 (sc)
ISBN: 978-1-4808-9048-0 (hc)
ISBN: 978-1-4808-9050-3 (e)

Library of Congress Control Number: 2020908394

Print information available on the last page.

Archway Publishing rev. date: 05/27/2020

To the immigrant children, victims of border politics. May you keep hope in your future and love in your heart.

CONTENTS

PART 4   TOOLS FOR A HAPPY JOURNEY

PART 5   THE JOURNEY CONTINUES

ACKNOWLEDGMENTS

Writing a book is an insurmountable adventure. Writing a memoir is doubly so, as it takes courage to relive the past, accept the present, and look forward to the future. It is a task that does not happen to one person alone in an empty room. It takes encouragement and support from those close enough to care.

I am fortunate to have a team of dear friends, some professionals in the field of publishing, and all avid readers who understand the process of translating thoughts and feelings to paper. I must first acknowledge Linda Gray, whom I nicknamed "Eagle Eye," for her expert editing of my second draft. In addition to her, and in no particular order, my appreciation goes to Dr. Deb Shaw, Sara Eyestone, the Reverend M. Catherine Volland, Dr. María Santamaría, Sandy Pitre, Saroj Baxter, Dr. Cindy Brenner, Judy Brooks, and Brenda Brooks. Their valuable comments and loving encouragement will forever be with me.

I would be remiss if I did not recognize the memory of my friends Lynn, Carmen, Elsa, and Penny, who have left us to claim their life reward. Their presence in my heart inspires me every day.

One last note of thanks goes to my daughter, Flori Bermúdez Oross, herself a wonderful photographer, for assisting me with the numerous photographs contained in this book. Every single image is a book in itself, and I greatly appreciate Flori's contribution.

Find a group of people who challenge and inspire you, spend a lot of time with them, and it will change your life.

—Amy Poehler

PREFACE

I wanted to entitle this book *Cuentos del Portal* (Stories from the Porch) to credit the source of most of the anecdotes I am sharing with you. In my day, our Havana porch was the center of our social interactions in the splendidly cool evenings. Several generations of family, friends and neighbors would congregate to share favorite tales, sometimes representing people who were no longer with us. This was a pleasurable way to get acquainted with the wisdom and wit of our ancestry, as well as to spend a joyful time together celebrating their lives.

I wanted to record the stories in a book so my grandchildren and their descendants would not miss the benefits of our legendary porch. Today, the practice has generally vanished, a victim of the high-tech world of communication and amusement, in addition to the unwelcome segregation members of different generations seek.

In the olden days, human beings were each other's entertainment and learning prospect. This tradition was also how generations passed on their values and mores to the young through face-to-face interactions. That is what *el portal* meant to me, and I lament its disappearance. My beloved grandchildren will have to be content with reading Nani's *One Immigrant in a World of Many: An American Story of Survival.*

Andrea Bermúdez
Santa Fe, New Mexico

PART I

THE BACKDROP FOR MY JOURNEY

CHAPTER 1

WHEN THE END BECOMES A BEGINNING

It was early morning in Havana when the household was awakened by the sound of insistent knocking and kicking on the front door. I still remember the day—Wednesday, February 4, 1959. My father was already awake and in his study, so he rushed to see what was happening. The rest of us were still in bed. Through the peephole, my anxious father could see three or four armed militia, rifles drawn, their demeanor irate. Heart pounding, he opened the door, and without a single word, the men pushed their way in.

"Move it," they finally said.

To my father's, "What is this all about?" they simply sneered.

The commotion woke everyone. My siblings and I froze in panic at the top of the stairs, while our mother ran downstairs to join my father. Tata and Carmen, our loyal, lifelong caretakers, stood by their rooms in total dismay, watching these men push furniture out of the way and throw our valuables around without any regard for the family. It was a home invasion, and we could not call the police, since they were the perpetrators.

Tata, my fearless nanny, finally faced the men without concern for her safety. Her family was being attacked. "What do you think you are doing here? This is a decent family who does nothing but good."

We finally learned that these men were searching for Batista's chief of the national police, Brigadier General Pilar García. My father, having recovered his composure, assured them that we did not even know the man and that he would not risk his family's safety for anyone. The men were unconvinced, and the hunt for García continued for several hours.

By this time in the revolution, many of Batista's close allies had either been executed or had fled the country. Since they were considered war criminals by Castro, aiding or abetting them was punishable by death or life imprisonment.

After taking apart our lower floor, the officers pushed their way upstairs, where my brothers and I stood like statues. The men aggressively pushed us out of the way with their guns and continued with their search. They looked in closets, under the beds, and inside of drawers. My mother followed them around protesting that García was too big to hide in those places. Father was concerned they would harm her, but quieting her now was hopeless.

A frustrating few hours had passed when the men finally gave up their search. There was devastation everywhere they had been. It felt like our home had become a war zone. Just as abruptly as the militia had arrived, they left with a very clear warning that all hope for our homeland was gone. We later found out General García had actually fled the country a month before, along with Batista and his close associates.

We never found out if this was a valid search or if it was meant to intimidate, but harassment did not end with this experience. Searches continued with regularity to remind us that we no longer belonged. The only thing left for us was to create a different future.

With great sadness, I was reminded of British novelist Raymond Chandler's words, "To say goodbye is to die a little." We had a tough choice now—saying goodbye to our homeland or facing a life with no future. That was the world I left behind.

Life's Journey: Flowers and Thorns

In the passage that ended when I left Cuba and restarted when I embraced the United States, there have been countless moments of joy, of grief, and of nothingness. I find that, of the three sorts, the hardest to endure is experiencing neither joy nor grief—emptiness robs our spirit without teaching us any significant lessons. With the passing of time, I have learned to appreciate the lessons that come from grief. I celebrate joyful moments and find ways to combat feelings of nothingness. I have tried to transform every end into a new beginning.

Overcoming Grief

In our journey, grief comes along to make us take notice of our joyful moments and to provide insight into what is really important in our lives. Some people escape grief, oftentimes through destructive means. Others face the music. The audacity to confront sorrow allows us to see through pain and unveil a message that often brings knowledge and growth.

The losses we experience make us the person we become and provide courage and strength to travel a more promising journey. It is important to revisit our losses to learn coping strategies that help us proceed into the future. My most serious losses happened early in my life. Among them, three stand out for me—the death of my oldest child, the passing of my parents, and the loss of my homeland. These three events taught me to embrace the present moment because the uncertain future may not be as good.

My most devastating loss was the death of my eldest son Peter, age twenty, in a tragic automobile accident. Nothing else in the world could be worse for a mother than having her child's life cut short. The need to remain sane, despite the guilt and the insurmountable sadness, gave me courage and purpose to look after my younger children, who were also grieving the loss. It was clear that I had to resolve the feeling of undeserved guilt and concentrate on helping my children cope. Facing pain is a critical step in the healing process. There is always room to grow if we make the space.

I came to realize that there was nothing I could have done to avoid the tragedy, so I accepted, with reluctance, that what had happened was our cross to bear. Pain slowly turned to happy memories of him—his youth, his zest for life, his beauty, his goodness, and his ability to make others laugh and celebrate. It helped me remember and be thankful for the last words he said to me, which were, "I am so proud of you mom." Three and a half decades after his passing, I realize that I owe Peter meaning and purpose in my life, and I am grateful that his loving presence has never left me.

My parents' demise was a different kind of loss. Both had lived a full life and fulfilled their promise, especially my father, who lived to be 101 years old. Despite recognizing these facts and acknowledging that the end comes to all, it is still difficult to imagine a life without your loved ones. Many times, I thought of sharing something with them, forgetting for an instant that they were gone. It is also a difficult realization that, when parents die, you become the generation on whom young ones depend for advice. You have, at this point, learned all that you can from your parents, and it becomes your responsibility to put those lessons into practice. Fortunately, there is much I learned from mine.

Having been born in the early 1900s, Mother was always ahead of her peers. Women of her generation did not pursue an education, as marriage and motherhood were their most important purposes in life. Mother had other ideas. When the four of us siblings were heading into adulthood, Mother decided to hire a tutor to finish the one subject she had left in her high school education—physics! Upon completing the course successfully, she enrolled at the university to pursue her love of American literature. Her interests culminated in the equivalent of a master's degree at the University of Havana. Equipped with credentials, she accepted a job as a principal of an English school in Cuba. What a role model for us!

Mother in the 1930's

Dreams, when made into plans, do happen. Or in Eleanor Roosevelt's words, "The future belongs to those who believe in the beauty of their dreams." Father was a physician by training and vocation. He started his new life as a political exile at age sixty-two. A man of character and dedication, he went on to become a well-respected member of a small eastern shore town in Maryland. Because the love of medicine was his core, Father was not able or willing to retire until age ninety-seven, as his patients insisted he continue his work.

Father, Dr. Carlos F. Barroso, MD circa 1928

It was not infrequent to hear a knock on the door by a parent bringing an injured child for my dad to treat. It was inspiring to see my father travel year after year to the Medical School of Georgia to complete requirements for his practice. It was not coincidental that his bright and promising oldest grandson, also named Carlos F. Barroso, was a medical student at that institution. Imagine the pleasure he must have felt attending seminars next to his grandchild, a future fourth generation MD!

My dad was a gigantic presence, despite being short in stature. He had the ability to entertain with his incredible war stories and wonderful sense of humor. I remember a visit to him when he had left a note for me on his door. The note had one of his infamous caricatures of an old man with a medical bag and a message, which read, "Gone to the nursing home, as a doctor, not a patient!" I realized that humor was one of his weapons against aging.

On his 101st birthday, he had a health crisis that required taking him to the hospital by ambulance. At some point he said, "I am so embarrassed." This showed me he was not worried or anxious, only uncomfortable showing weakness. While waiting for the ambulance, I put my arms around him without saying anything. I just wanted him to know I was there. He looked at me and said, "This is it, you know. Don't worry about me; don't be sad. I am excited to start my new chapter." Those words have never left me.

Few people have direct experience with tornados, earthquakes, or hurricanes, but through media, we have all witnessed the devastation they cause. Hardly ever do we compare those losses with victims of revolution or war.

Castro Happens

In 1959, a Communist revolution took the reins of government in Cuba. Many thousands, including myself and members of my immediate family, sought exile in foreign lands. My family was fortunate to choose the United States to start life anew. I had gotten married two weeks before our departure, resulting in my husband and I having to leave loved ones and valued possessions behind. The fear of never seeing my parents, family, or friends again was overwhelming. Fortunately, after several years apart, most of the family was reunited. The same cannot be said about my friends, as I never saw most of them again. Learning to not look back and not wish reality were different were perhaps two of the most useful lessons learned from that experience.

When grief becomes a memory rather than a presence, we are ready to continue our journey. We also never know when or where we are going to encounter a significant survival message. A recent posting in social media by Purple Clover imparted a profound lesson to overcome grief. "Let it hurt. Let it bleed. Let it heal. Let it go."

Attaining Joy

Moments of joy are only abundant in our lives if we take the time to acknowledge and celebrate them. For so many, the belief of a glass half-empty impedes their ability to see the blessings they have received in life. I am grateful for the memories—as reminders of my good fortune and providers of the energy behind my meaningful journey.

Although joy appears self-explanatory, achieving and maintaining joyfulness requires attitude. I define joy as acceptance, contentment, and celebration of the present. Having your first child, falling in love, and achieving dreams are obviously moments to celebrate and feel joyful. To me, it is more important to find joy in the simple moments—a bird's song, a puppy's love, a good book, a conversation with a friend. If we focus with intent on those instances and disregard any thoughts that disrupt our contentment, we increase the likelihood of attaining a joyful state.

To this day, I still remember when my dad came home with a red and blue scooter, a present for my third birthday. The feeling of excitement returns, when I think of my loyal Tata and me waiting for my dad's arrival. I also remember the large package, which I managed to tear to shreds and expose the much-awaited scooter. I was so overjoyed, although the wooden wheels allowed it to only move at a turtle's pace. This poignant memory makes me smile every time. Simple thoughts and memories sometimes buffer life's challenges and fill us with the promise of better times ahead.

Many people spend a lifetime in search of the elusive feeling of happiness by pursuing significant or costly ventures. If we could thread our joyful moments into a memory chain, we reach a stage of contentment and acceptance for what we have. My mantra, "It is what it is," has helped me see the uselessness of wishing that our present moment were different. Making the best of what we have lets us appreciate who we are and what we have accomplished in our lives.

Feeling Emptiness

The most damaging challenge to a joyful state is experiencing "nothingness." We have reached it when we feel the world around us is static and oppressive. We are looking at walls with a "no way out" sign. This can happen when people stop pursuing interests, friendships, and dreams. What better antidote than surrounding ourselves with those very experiences that we try to avoid. I strongly believe that developing interests is conducive to good mental health. If it seems like a chore at first, connecting ourselves with enjoyable activities or people can be very helpful in filling the empty shell. Friends, pets, and nature in general are also effective means to make our dark tunnels temporary.

Although I consider my thirties to have been years of crisis, the challenges taught me much about rebirth and survival. Hitting bottom is, in many ways, a critical juncture in being reborn. When we face difficult times, we develop character, a trait required to survive life's ordeals. We would never be happy if we had never been sad. The decade of my thirties made possible my rebirth in my forties and fifties, when I started to fulfill my promise as a person.

Our life journeys are challenging, but our attitudes can make them joyful by living in the moment, filling our cup with positive memories, and learning from the sad moments. The nature of our journey can be changed, if we consider grief a temporary state that teaches us important lessons, and if we replace nothingness with meaningful interests and distractions. My father said it best. "Life is an attitude."

My Mission in Life

I thought that, having been born in the eventful year of 1941, I had inherited the responsibility to make a difference. It marked the entrance of the United States into World War II and its participation in all the tragic events that went hand in hand with war. Our president at the time was Franklin Delano Roosevelt, who served a record of four consecutive presidencies and made history in so many other ways. In response to the Great Depression, he had initiated the New Deal, which included social security, among several other programs aimed at providing federal relief to the unemployed and the poor. Also in 1941, the first Disney movie, *Dumbo*, was released; Mount Rushmore's drilling was completed; and a law was passed to make Thanksgiving an official celebration on the fourth Thursday of every November.

Since I was born in Havana, Cuba, and my family was living on the island at the time, we only witnessed these events from a distance. The United States eventually became our home, so we claim its history as part of our roots. To magnify the importance of my birth year, Easter Sunday fell on April 13, the day I was born. Those events reinforced my belief that my mission had to be consequential. As I look back on my life events, it is hard for me to judge whether I can claim any positive impact on anyone else's life. It is not always clear to us what bearing we have had on the lives of others, so all we can do is be our best, considering the circumstances.

As a mother, I have given life to three children whose journeys I have definitively shaped. As a teacher, there are students whose lives I have touched. I can't help but feel a sense of regret that, when raising my children, I was not aware of the influence my words and actions could have on their psyches. There are many times when I see myself in what they decide to do and hear my voice in what they say or think. I want them to know I did the best I could, hoping that my love for them would be evident in their hearts.

To assuage my remorse, I keep telling myself that circumstances dictate our actions, and having done the best I could at the time is all that is humanly possible. In addition, nature has to be considered in these matters, so the genetic make-up of our children has a significant impact on their futures. Just as we cannot claim their successes, we should not blame ourselves for their missteps.

Peter, Flori and E.J. with my father (Abuelo) in 1966

With regards to my students, I have had signs that show me I had an impact on their lives. One student, also a teacher, stopped me once and let me know that she had a quote of mine posted in her classroom, to remind her students about the importance of human diversity and equality. I could not remember the words she cited and often wondered if they had even been mine originally!

To the point, my having been a messenger had been meaningful to her and was important enough to pass the message on.

Another student visited me to let me know she had not long to live as a result of cancer spreading in her body. She came to thank me for giving her a direction in life when she most needed it and for helping her select a profession that had made her feel valuable. She graduated that summer, only to succumb to her illness a short time later. Her powerful message of appreciation has continued to inspire me to this day.

A few years ago, after my retirement from the University of Houston-Clear Lake, three of my former students, now educators in their own right, invited me to speak at an event at the university. I was curious to see how they had continued to lead projects that I had started. Little did I know the event was in my honor to present me with the "Starfish Award." The place was packed with a mixture of familiar and new faces.

When one of my students came to the podium, she asked the audience to raise their hands if they had been my students. Many did. Then she asked how many more had been, in any way, affected by those who had raised their hands. Remarkably, the rest of the audience joined. I cannot express my feelings at the time, as tears of humility tested my composure.

Another of my students explained that the award had been named for the starfish's ability to regenerate limbs and regrow a new organism. My students were giving me permission to claim my part in their success. I had never felt more rewarded professionally than at that moment.

We all know that we have at least one mission to accomplish, and whether we do or don't accomplish it may not ever be known by us. Sometimes, there are simple moments that remind us of what we mean to others, allowing us to recognize that we do have a place in this world. Our next generation philosopher-entertainer, seven-year-old grandson Max, recently told me, "Nani, I love you to the moon and back. When you die, I am going to cry so much!"

Through Max's words, I become aware of the value of my own existence. If we act in concert with our true selves and do not get distracted by the perceptions of others, we have a better chance to feel "mission accomplished" at the end of our days.

Keeping Up with the Changing Times

Our journeys are now taking place in a highly technological environment, which requires constant learning and adaptation. Along with the advancement of technology comes a radical change in our culture and our language. In the olden days, the elderly were responsible for passing on values and mores, which served as survival tools for the next generation. Since it was the older generation who possessed the knowledge and skills to function in the world, they were considered the wise and knowledgeable generation.

Today, change happens fast as new versions of the phone or tablet are constantly being unveiled. Each version requires new knowledge and skills, so if I don't change and adapt, I am simply left behind in virtual blindness. Wisdom alone no longer serves as a survival tool. Knowledge and skills are essential, but there has been a reversal in how they are transferred. Rather than me passing on to my descendants the secrets of survival, they are the ones who have the ability to steer in the world of technology. It is my grandchildren who are empowered to teach me how to survive.

My grandparents' generation witnessed the first telephone and the first radio. My parents witnessed the development of aviation as a means of transport. My generation saw the first color television and walked on the moon. The next generations are witnessing momentous changes on a daily basis, creating the infrastructure for an entirely new world with different challenges and rewards. Youth is in charge of the know-how, but we are responsible to keep up with the times.

As I discuss how times have changed with my grandchildren, even the youngest laughs when I tell him how the first computers worked in my generation. They cannot believe that they were huge pieces of equipment that resided in rooms or laboratories. Students used them exclusively for statistical or math calculations for a graduate thesis or a doctoral dissertation. There were no word processors, and typewriters were used to transcribe text.

My dissertation in 1974 was typed by a professional, who charged sixty-five cents per page. Since there were no hard disks that could save files, she kept her work in a refrigerator in case of fire! Any changes were drastic, as the project had to be retyped at a cost per page. My friend and colleague Paul Wagner lost his dissertation when driving with a window open! It literally flew out the window, and he had to start all over again from his notes.

My mother's older sister, Niní, and husband Tato had one of the first color TVs in the Havana of the fifties. Friday night was an event, as family, friends, and neighbors descended upon them to watch live wrestling (*lucha libre*). El Chiclayano (a famous Peruvian wrestler) against

La Amenaza Roja (The Red Menace) would create standing room only in my aunt and uncle's living room. The gathering was most enjoyable, and it gave us a chance to live in community. I was considered privileged because I could watch television any time during my frequent visits, and I certainly had an attention-grabbing topic to share with my classmates the next day. In the world of today, a substantial majority of Americans own at least one television set, so my experience in the fifties would be far from noteworthy.

Social media is our venue to communicate with others. Facebook, Twitter, Instagram, texts, and emails have expanded our number of "friends" but have greatly diminished our degree of intimacy. We now have a president who enjoys governing by "tweets." Messages travel far and swiftly, which often creates chaos and misunderstandings. The world is our audience, so communicating person to person by letter is becoming obsolete. The internet has replaced our porches, living rooms, rotary phones, and letters as media for interacting with others. We have become less deliberate and more impulsive in our effort to keep up with the fast-changing world around us.

As innovations advance, changes in language are expected. New words enter the vocabulary, such as *texting, emoji, terabytes, Wi-Fi, online*, and so on. And new behaviors develop as well. It is not infrequent to see a table of four at a restaurant, where each individual is interacting with his or her phone, rather than with the others at the table. It is no wonder that we no longer speak in complete sentences. Our text messages use words such as *TY, YW, LOL,* and *LMAO.* For individuals in my generation, it takes some adjustment. If I had said the word that the A in LMAO stands for as a child, I would have had my mouth washed out with soap.

We used to play games that we invented, so we not only socialized and participated, but also created. Today's youth plays games created by others, often violent, where problem solving seems to have replaced pleasure. "Technology makes our lives easier," some people say. And I disagree. We have gained in productivity at the price of an ever-present learning curve, but we end up doing more in less time. We have also lost privacy. Visiting websites leaves a footprint, and "they" always find you. I don't really know who "they" are, but I have the feeling they live with us. Most recently, I have noticed "their" presence in my car. The navigation not only tells me where I am and where I am going but also the speed limit required for the area. I don't know whether to be scared or grateful that I am alive and functioning in such a tech-rich environment. No one knows where the future is taking us, but wherever it is, we are going full speed.

CHAPTER 2

HOME SWEET HOME

To my generation, parents were superheroes to be kept on a pedestal. This belief forced them to play the role to perfection, so they kept their human frailties to themselves. You knew them mostly as a category, "parents," not as individuals who breathe, worry, and make mistakes. I feel a great sense of loss, in that I never really got to know them.

My parents were a great team. Father was always provider in chief, and Mother was the decision-maker. Their lives were challenging, but their strength of character and sense of humor allowed them to celebrate moments of bliss and endure trials with grace and dignity.

My Father

When I think of my father, I think of his pride, strength, humor, intelligence, and incredible knowledge. Until his last days at 101, father studied with diligence, retaining vast amounts of his favorite topics—medicine and history. As children, my father and his younger brother would reenact famous Napoleonic wars in their Havana yard with their toy soldiers. A connoisseur of military history, he could identify country and rank by just looking at a uniform. You would not want to be sitting next to him at a movie if a military figure appeared, because he would point out everything that was wrong in the rendering.

Born on March 8, 1900, in Unión de Reyes, Cuba, a small town in the beautiful province of Matanzas, he was the oldest child born to Dr. Fabián Barroso and Dulce María Piñar.

Carlos Fabián Barroso Piñar at six months

My father was a product of his generation. A conservative Catholic, he could not help but be a defender of the established mores and values his culture represented. His father, although a physician by training, was a sugar industrialist. Sixteen years his wife's senior, my grandfather Fabián towered over her, at six foot to her four foot eleven.

Grandparents Dulce Piñar and Fabián Barroso

Mamaquico, as her family nicknamed her, was petite, redheaded, and blue-eyed with a very regal demeanor. Many compared her beauty to Gloria Swanson, a Hollywood star of the silent film era. Mamaquico's upbringing was privileged as the daughter of a wealthy sugar mill owner, the Central Flora, as well as an arable farm, Babiney. Known for her extravagance in later years, she once removed her expensive diamond earrings and placed them in her church's collection plate.

Father and his three siblings, Margarita, Jorge, and Haydée, were homeschooled by a tutor. Every morning, Mamaquico would come into the classroom and write a proverb on the blackboard, along the lines of, *"Un lugar para cada cosa y cada cosa en su lugar"* (a place for everything and everything in its place). This task was her contribution to the day's lesson. My father thought it was somewhat humorous that the class would not start without the daily ritual.

As a child at Babiney, father grew up fond of trains, and he would not miss the train's comings and goings, an affection that accompanied him through life. I remember that every home in which he lived as an adult had a room dedicated to his model trains. He was able to offset the stressful work of a physician by allowing his inner child to play and be creative. Father would spend hours building little towns and letting his train travel through picturesque places his vivid imagination had created. He favored dressing up in a three-piece suit, but sometimes his dapper looks were marred by a paint stain, a giveaway that he had taken time to play with his trains.

At age twenty-five, Father graduated from the School of Medicine at the University of Havana, a profession that made the man. As a physician, he briefly became a medical captain in the Cuban army, yet he was far from being an authoritarian figure. Moneymaking was not his motivation; helping others was his calling. His patients were diverse, and each of them was as important as any other. Some were poor fishermen, who lived by the Almendares River. They received my father's best care to make them well. Sometimes they could not pay for the visit, a fact that did not matter to my father. It was common for him to come home with a cake or a pie given by a patient who could not afford to reimburse my father's work. It was clear he was devoted to his profession and to his family, but decisions regarding the children were left to my mother.

He was never far from his books, his most precious possession. During a phone conversation in his late nineties, I asked him what he was doing, and his response was, "Studying."

Father at a 100-years old in Hurlock, Maryland

I am blessed that my father lived to be older than a century. As a result, I had more opportunities to get to know the real man. I think I was the apple of his eye, but each one of my three siblings felt he was. Somewhere I read that this was a sign of successful parenting.

Father also maintained hospital privileges until his eighties. He always told the story that that it was the hospital practice to have its doctors assigned to various committees that would become active in the event of a disaster. Toward the end, my father was invited to join the "Morgue Committee." His explanation was, "Since from there, I can't do any harm." Having the ability to laugh at himself, he took every event in life with humor. Father remained a widower after Mother's passing, and became fiercely self-reliant, preferring to live at home on his own.

He was able to maintain independence until age ninety-nine, when his unmarried son retired and joined him in Hurlock, Maryland.

My grandparents' families had been friends before my parents ever met. Two years younger than my father, Mother remembers visiting his home when she was five or six years old. A young boy playing with trains caught her eye. Little did they know then that, sixteen years later, destiny would link their lives for more than fifty years. Their first meeting was a bit unusual but no doubt meant to be. When my mother's father, José Manuel García-Lavín, was near death, Mamaquico asked my father to check on her friend's health. As father arrived at the home, he found that my grandfather had just passed away, so he left the house before meeting the family.

A month later on August 6, 1923, Mamaquico asked my father again to visit with my mother's family and offer her condolences. The announcement that a young, marriageable medical student was coming for a visit propelled girls in the family to dress up and look attractive—that is all the girls except my mother, who could not have cared less. She eventually appeared in the living room looking very casual and eating a piece of toast. He thought she was the most beautiful young woman he had ever seen, and her unpretentious ways charmed him.

A few days after the visit, one of Mother's cousins eventually got tired of my father's frequent phone calls and finally told him, "Carlos, I know who you really want to talk to, so here she is on the phone."

Their courtship was not routine. Always under the vigilant eye of a chaperone, they would go for a stroll in the park. Mother says that they would look back and see five or six members of the family following them.

Never disrespectful of the early 1900's customs, Father would not leave the house without wearing the typical flat-brimmed straw hat. One day, while riding the train to see her, the wind took his hat, leaving him with the embarrassment of being seen hatless in public. I am sure his humiliation doubled when my mother saw him not wearing one. He used to tell us, it was almost as bad as having forgotten to wear a shirt!

Three years later, on September 22, 1926, Medical Lieutenant Carlos Fabián Barroso married Dulce María García Lavín at the Iglesia Parroquial de la Habana. The young couple moved to Holguín, where he would soon be promoted to captain.

Dulce María García-Lavín y González on her wedding day

His military career was cut short by the 1933 Batista Revolution. Father was imprisoned at the Hotel Nacional, a five-star hotel, normally a tourist destination. Rumor had it that he had been killed in the fracas, so two of my uncles went to the morgue on a fact-finding visit. Fortunately for us, the rumor was untrue, and Mother, who was caring for her five-year old son, was protected from the gossip.

My parents and brother Carlos, Jr.

Their life outside the military resumed two months after captivity, when Father was freed to join the family. He went into private practice and eventually joined Dr. Cándido Hoyos as a lung specialist treating tuberculosis and other respiratory ailments. He enjoyed great success with his patients, and many felt they owed their lives to my father. One of them, a beautiful young lady who had been cured of tuberculosis, asked him to walk her down the aisle on her wedding day.

By then my little brother, Rod, and I were about four and six respectively, so Mother took us to the ceremony. Rod was almost in tears, and Mother noticed that he kept caressing her, while saying something she could not understand. She asked him what was going on, to which he responded, "You are prettier than she is." Only then, did Mother realize that Rod thought my father was getting married to someone else!

The School of Medicine, from which Father had graduated, invited him to teach pharmacology, which he did for many decades. He hand-wrote a single book in the 1970s dealing with the subject and gave it to his eldest grandson, Carlos III, fourth in line medical doctor. The young physician was proud of his grandfather's unconditional dedication to his career. As stated earlier, when father had to attend yearly medical training because of his age, he would do so at the same school that his grandson was attending.

In late 1961, Father left Cuba for exile in the United States. By then, it was clear that Castro was in complete control of the government, and a future there was unlikely. Three of his children had already left, and Mother and son Fernando's chance to leave was coming soon. Cubans had to leave when the opportunity arose, and Father could not afford the luxury of waiting for Mother and Fernando to get their turn.

There was a moment of suspense at the José Martí Airport in Havana the day he left. His passport did not indicate that he was a physician, since this professional class was not allowed to leave the country. Father felt apprehensive when he recognized the immigration official checking passports as one of his former patients. Fortunately, the man's loyalty to his old doctor won out, and he allowed Father to board the plane without any objections.

At the time, my oldest brother Carlos was leaving a post at the Western State Hospital in Staunton, Virginia, to work on a urology residency. He thought he could negotiate Father's future employment. But first, Father had to pass the foreign board exam to be able to practice medicine in the United States. His conversational English was modest, but his medical vocabulary was up to par, as he'd spent his life pouring over textbooks written in English. He aced the exam, and moved with newly arrived Mother and second son, Fernando, to Virginia. The hospital offered a home on its beautiful grounds as a part of the contract.

My son, Peter, was born in Miami, Florida, on March 3, 1962, and instantly became my parents' pride. By May, we were also moving to Virginia to live with them. Those were joyful years, as the family was together again after years of separation. Peter would go crazy when *Abuelo* (Grandpa) came home from work, and, with Peter in his stroller, the two would take long walks together on the hospital grounds. Mother, in the meantime, was learning to cook and keep house, which she approached with enthusiasm. Dinner was always a surprise, sometimes better than others, but always showing Mother's ability to be creative.

In 1964, the state of Maryland opened the doors to Cuban physicians who had a track record of practicing and teaching in their country to go into private practice. My father applied and was given the opportunity. It was hard for us to part again, but we knew that this step was important for the family. Father's job at the Western State Hospital had opened doors for us as well. My ex-husband and brother were attending the University of Virginia, and I eventually received scholarships at Mary Baldwin College, Randolph Macon Woman's College, and the University of Virginia. My father was always the provider, *el horcón* (the supporter), as I called him. He strongly believed in giving to others, which obviously included helping all of his children pursue a future.

During the Hurlock, Maryland, years my parents' lives read like a storybook. They bought a red brick colonial home on Main Street and created a haven for my children's summer vacations. Their house was always filled with family visitors, who would not miss an opportunity to be with them. My parents established themselves as respected members of the community. The City of Hurlock provided a medical center for his practice as the sole physician for the city and its adjacent towns. On holiday parades, Father frequently served as the grand marshal. Everyone knew my parents and loved them—to the point that, once, Father lost his Havana cigar on the street, and it was returned to his mailbox!

Mother also learned to drive in her sixties, and she was always first in making fun of her skill, or lack thereof. She would often tell people that, when you arrived in Maryland, her home state, there was a freeway sign that read, "Beware of Dulce." It was not uncommon for my father to have to call AAA to get Mother's car out of trouble, since parallel parking, among other skills, had never been totally mastered. As a matter of fact, the officer who passed her on her second attempt made her promise she would never try to parallel park again. She still found great pleasure in her no-frills 1966 brown and tan Buick.

In 1976, Mother had a health crisis, and open-heart surgery was indicated. Father worried that she would suffer a sudden death when a heart valve failed. He brought her to my home in Houston, where well-known surgeons and cardiologists could further address her condition. Father had kept her alive for so many years, but he felt that medications had gone as far as they could, and now their interactions had begun to work against Mother. Surgery was her last chance to recover. Unfortunately, in the 1970s, valve replacement surgery was still in its infancy, and Mother passed away on December 11, 1976.

Father moved back to his much-loved Hurlock, Maryland, which had been home to them for so many years. He lived alone, continued his practice, and refused to give up his home filled with happy memories. We respected the man. So all his children accepted his desire for independence.

Among the many things he had to learn in the twenty-five years he lived as a widower was cooking for himself. On one of my visits, he offered to fix me a tuna sandwich that, according to him, was scrumptious. As I opened the cupboard, I noticed five cans of tuna—cat food. Fortunately, these had been bought on sale the day before, and he had not yet used them. In time, he actually became a pretty good cook, with a very limited menu.

A family reunion for his hundredth birthday made us feel grateful to have had him as a father and role model for so long. Father's children, grandchildren, siblings, in-laws, friends, and patients, gathered to honor the man who had given us so much. He was the center of attention on his big birthday, and he enjoyed himself with glee.

Father celebrating his 100th birthday with his grandchildren Flori, E.J. Rod, Carlos III, Mario and Maria Dolores and his great grandchildren John Paul, Audrey, Carlos IV, Joseph, Mathew, Nathaniel and Michael

Everyone wanted to be with him, listen to his war stories, and watch him dance to a rhythm that had nothing to do with the music that was playing. It did not matter. A man who had always lived life to the fullest was having fun and making his guests thankful for the moment. In celebrating with him, we were reminded to find meaning in all we do, to never stop looking for humor, and to never look back. As we repeatedly heard him say, "If you fall from the horse, get back on and ride forward."

Dr. Carlos F. Barroso's 100th birthday picture

His next birthday was to be his last. A crisis developed during the celebration, and we had to call an ambulance. When he shared with me his embarrassment, I responded, "Why should you be embarrassed? Everyone needs a little help every once in a while." He just smiled, but he knew his end was near. He was not afraid. He was excited, just like Barrie's Peter Pan—"To die will be an awfully big adventure." I did not see a feeble man contemplating his end. I saw a giant, whose memory would always serve to inspire me to never give up.

On July 19, 2001, Father made his transition. The funeral cortege took him and his family around Hurlock, his city, where the townsfolk stood silently in the streets paying homage to their beloved Dr. Barroso. He had loved his people, and they had loved him. Military and police saluted the hearse as we traveled toward his final place of rest. In a book, *Images of America: Dorchester County*, Father is recognized in the chapter "Those who Served." The office building in which he practiced was renamed Barroso Medical Center. A plaque appears at its entrance: "Dedicated in 1993 in honor of Carlos F. Barroso, MD, in recognition for his many years of exemplary service to the citizens of North Dorchester." A passenger train at the Hurlock station also carries the name "Dr. Carlos F. Barroso, MD," and his grandchildren and great-grandchildren were proud to be on its first run.

Glimpses of My Mother

Despite being born with heart issues, my mother, as I recall, rarely ever sat down. My first image of her is that of a person in constant motion and animated chatter, going places. She was always on the go, ready for a new adventure. It seemed to me she never walked; instead, she ran.

Mother was born in the city of Cárdenas to José Manuel García-Lavín Borges and Andrea González Amaro. She was the youngest of nine children and, as such, became the center of her family life.

Grandparents Jose Manuel García-Lavín and Andrea González

Mother's father owned Central Dos Rosas, a large-scale sugar mill in northwest Cárdenas, in the province of Matanzas, considered the birthplace of the Cuban sugar industry. In the 1880s, Cuba was a prosperous sugar producer and trader. The boom continued into the next century, followed by the Great Depression. The prosperity enjoyed by the García-Lavíns came to an end, and the family moved to Havana, where Mother and her siblings were to meet their future spouses.

Grandfather became the administrator of another sugar mill, Central Perseverancia. Sadly, their oldest daughter, Nena, died in 1919 of tuberculosis at the renowned Adirondack Cottage Sanatorium in Saranac Lake, New York. Sometimes, losses seem to follow losses. A son, Ramón (Tío Moncito) was kidnapped for ransom along with my grandfather, and both eventually were freed. The ransom further depleted their declining fortune. On July 11, 1923, José Manuel García Lavín passed away. It was the family's fortitude that helped them to overcome their grief and strengthen their indelible bond.

Mother was a beautiful woman, whose jet-black eyes (*ojos de azabache*) revealed her keen intelligence. Born on November 18, 1902,

Mother broke every rule of her generation. She was independent, a university graduate, and an employed professional. Her environment growing up was dictated by strict Catholic norms. In the hierarchy, women were meant for service, marriage, and motherhood. Working outside the home was less acceptable than domestic bliss.

Dulce García-Lavín de Barroso

In defying this dictum by obtaining a degree to work as a teacher and principal, Mother made her children proud. Her achievements became an inspiration for us and an example to be emulated. A strong advocate for education, Mother went to great lengths to ensure her children would have the best schooling. My three brothers became a surgeon, a lawyer, and an engineer, and I relinquished architecture to become a university professor and administrator.

Mother's two pet peeves were rodents and age. Age was not a topic of discussion with her. As a matter of fact, she did not celebrate her birthdays, for fear people would find out how old she was. It took until we read her obituary to solve the mystery of her age. I remember when she was recuperating from open-heart surgery at my home in Houston, and I asked her where she kept her insurance card. With a determined "don't ask me why" look, she told me I could find it in a small envelope in her purse that said, "Prayers to St. Jude." There, she kept all the cards that had her birth date. Obviously, she thought no one would be interested in examining this envelope, and out of respect, I didn't either, although curiosity was killing me. I still feel I never knew her as a person. How did she feel about life, her marriage, her politics, her children? I have always lived with these questions. I know she loved us, but did she like us?

When Mother's father passed away, she was twenty-three years old. She remained very close to her mother, Andrea, whom I never had the chance to meet. I was named after her, since she passed away on Saint Anne's Day, the name mother had originally chosen for her first daughter. She spoke lovingly about her mother's wisdom, a trait she definitely inherited. Abuela Andreíta, as she was lovingly called by her grandchildren, taught her girls, by example, to be strong and independent and stand their ground for what they believed. These traits were passed on to the next generations, when granddaughters Silvia, Gloria, Lourdes, and Andrea would someday let the world know they counted.

Brother Carlos with our grandmother Andrea in 1931

There was nothing Mother and her siblings enjoyed more than a good argument, which sometimes got quite heated. I remember witnessing one, which centered on the number of Atlanta's residents. It did not matter what subject, the passion and enjoyment were there. I find it very difficult to chronicle my mother, a person who defied description by leading a life that, although short, can only be recounted as a whirl-wind. She never lived to be as old as I am now, but she managed to raise four children; graduate from the University of Havana; work as both a principal and a teacher; celebrate her fiftieth wedding anniversary; and live a productive life in exile.

Born with a quick wit, she could always generate a humorous come-back. On a walk with a dear friend, who could be described as handsome with a generous body size and beautiful blond hair, the pair ran into a man who stopped to admire the young ladies. He could not help himself from saying, "The mother is more beautiful than the daughter." Not being shy in setting things straight, she turned to the man and said, "Mister, you insulted us both. You called her *vieja* (old) and me *fea* (ugly)."

People enjoyed her company. She exuded energy and *joie de vivre,* although her health was compromised from birth. Mother was born with a defective tricuspid heart valve, a fact that did not stop her from living life to the fullest. Canasta was one of her favorite pastimes, and she enjoyed many afternoons playing with her good friends Leonor, Nilda, and sister-in-law Aurora. It seemed to me that she was always *en route* somewhere, purse in hand, rushing out the door.

Without being extravagant, mother enjoyed a closet full of purple dresses of every conceivable shade. Shoes were also a weakness, although she seemed to favor a single pair, which she wore for every occasion. She never wore pants, T-shirts, or tennis shoes. She seemed to be dressed up from dawn to dusk! She expected as much from me, although I failed her in that regard.

Her tastes were simple. Her preferred restaurant was Eat's on the Eastern Shore of Maryland. When my siblings and I would visit, we preferred Father to invite us, as he always chose the country club over my mother's favorite truck stop. Her meal of choice was Maryland's famous blue crab, and she always carried claw crackers in her purse, just in case.

During one of my visits, I bought a dozen crabs to share with my parents. My mother and I sat across from each other and started sharing our portion of the crabs while we visited. She had said earlier, "Let's save half for your dad and enjoy the rest." As time passed and our enjoyable conversation continued, we kept reducing the number of crabs to save for Dad, until Mother finally said, "We don't need to save any for your father. I don't think he likes them that much." With that said, we ate the rest. These treasured memories have enriched my days.

Mother adapted well to exile. After a brief stint during her sixties teaching high school English and Spanish in Staunton, Virginia, she retired to the life of a physician's wife on the Eastern Shore of Maryland. She learned to enjoy new activities she had never thought of pursuing. She joined the garden club, turned into a stamp and coin collector, and became a fan of TV game shows. Mother loved English and kept a notebook with new words that she would learn from her small screen experience. She would practice her new vocabulary when she talked to me later in the day. I could always tell what she had been up to when she would say things such as, "She had a plethora of things to do"—a total giveaway!

Mother even tried sewing, but that did not last. She felt she could improve on patterns, making them easier to follow, with little or no success. Armed with newspapers, she would draw her own pattern for a robe. It had a front and a back, although the sleeves were long and continuous. It would have worked if it weren't for the fabric congregating under her armpits. The experience discouraged her from pursuing this hobby further.

My mother died a month after her seventy-fourth birthday from heart surgery complications. She had lived a more sedentary life than she would have wanted, but her demeanor concealed her frail health. Her vivacious personality and wittiness made her a family favorite, a character. My mother lived her life in defiance of a "can't do" attitude. She taught me that all is possible, if I can only find a way to pursue it. Her trademark was that she always found a way. She went too soon, but her days were lived with intensity and purpose.

I have great admiration for both of my parents for having been able to adapt so well to life in exile. They survived leaving all that was known to them—homeland, family, and value systems—to pursue a new beginning in a very different world. They never gave up or complained. They never looked back with a yearning for what was lost. They simply lived a new meaningful life and, by example, helped all four of their adult children to do the same.

My Brothers

Being the oldest son, Carlos inherited the unspoken responsibility of following the rules of patrimony. He became a physician, married a girl from a "good Catholic" family, and had four wonderful children.

My brother Carlos and I

As a urologist, my brother was able to invent new techniques in surgery, including sex reassignment. He was unable to continue this type of surgery, as his youngest son was bullied unmercifully by his classmates because his father "turned men into women." One of Carlos's innovations was a type of suture that saved time and complications. He attributed his contribution to medical research to our grandmother Andreíta, who taught him how to crochet when he was six or seven.

Despite my brother's success as a surgeon, his life was filled with tragedy. Carlos's oldest son, Carlos III, became an anesthesiologist, following in his elders' footsteps. A rising star in his chosen field, my nephew tragically lost his life at age forty-nine, a victim of an aneurysm. Mario Enrique, my brother's second son, a happily married father of three sons, also lost his life at the same age from lung cancer. These losses changed my brother's personality, and his detachment from the rest of the world became more evident. Carlos spent his last years contemplating the fact that he ran through life without savoring all the gifts he was granted. At eighty-three, my oldest bother passed away from COPD complications, the result of a lifelong smoking habit.

Born in 1934, Fernando was second in line. Always studious, quiet, not too athletic, and extremely religious, he was the polar opposite of his rambunctious older brother. As the middle child, he was unable to attract enough attention to himself.

Mother with Carlos and Fernando circa 1936

For many years, he and I could not communicate, as there were few subjects we could agree on. Interestingly, we both chose nineteenth-century Spanish literature as an area of concentration during our graduate studies at the University of Virginia, except he chose the conservative Catholic authors, while I favored the liberal ones.

He never married, but his nephews and nieces became his progeny. They adored "Uncle Tuty" and he, in turn, adored them. His life is meaningful, with his church; his books; and his interest in opera, theatre, and movies. Now, in his eighties, he drives himself ninety minutes across the Chesapeake Bay Bridge to attend cultural activities in the nation's capital. When my father turned ninety-nine, Fernando retired as a professor of Spanish literature from James Madison University, and he went to live with our father in the family home, where he remains to this day.

What drives my only living brother is an overblown interpretation of Catholicism, which controls his thoughts and behavior. Fernando's views on the role of men and women in society reflect the male-dominated values promulgated by the church. We have had serious arguments regarding his stringent views of sin and salvation, feminism, and politics. On a spectrum, we each occupy an opposing extreme. Fernando can't or won't bend, listen, or change the views he has held all his life, which feeds in me a stubborn determination not to change my mind either. Those who disagree with him are wrong and will have to face damnation at the end of the road.

Fernando has made it clear that he does not approve of my choices in life, but I am sure he is praying for my salvation. While he has chosen to hang on to the past, I infrequently look back, as, in my world, the best is still to come. After our parents and siblings' passing, we have been left behind to mend our relationship. Fortunately, we have both learned to avoid the main subjects of disagreement—gender, religion, and politics. We are closer now than we ever were.

The youngest child, Rodrigo, was born in 1942, just twenty months after me. He was likely a genius but with a sense of humor. When Rod was four years of age, Mother found him sitting on the floor staring into space. She became a bit concerned and asked what he was thinking. He looked at her and smiled, "I was thinking that today is the yesterday of tomorrow." Mother realized quickly that there was no reason for worry. Her little boy's brilliance was beginning to emerge.

Mother and Rod in 1943

Rod and I were very close as children, since we were also close in age. We enjoyed "pretend" games, such as having a real job. A turkey crate turned into an office was our favorite fantasy game. The fact that we could not stand up did not deter our busy work.

At five years old, Rod tended to overplay his business savvy, a fact that got him in trouble sometimes, such as the time when he decided to pass around a can to collect money from my mother's party guests. Needless to say, she made him go back to apologize and return the donations. He had felt justified since he had seen it done in church on Sundays. This event caused Mother to die of embarrassment, but it showed Rod's enterprising nature. If you could use a few words to describe Rod, it would most likely be brilliant and very funny, but he was also generous, loving, accepting, creative, spiritual, thoughtful, unique, and passionate.

Rod was married twice and had a son who inherited his dad's sense of humor. My brother became an electrical engineer, and devoted his professional life to designing computer chips. A serious fall at work injured the frontal lobe of his brain, and his ability to function was compromised. The accident forced him to retire, and move to a nursing home in Melbourne, Florida, where he spent the rest of his days.

It was a tough experience to visit my "little brother" at the nursing home. It was more my apprehension than his reality. He was at peace, even telling me, "I am fine here. This is home." Rod had a laptop opened to one of his intricate artistic creations, which he showed us with pride and excitement. Although Rod was surrounded by patients with various stages of dementia, his mood was upbeat and his conversation logical and animated. His health was declining, but his positive attitude was not. Rod passed away on November 3, 2014. Part of his obituary read:

> His family remembers him as a precocious little boy who was loved by everyone who met him. He spent his professional career as an Electrical Engineer, but at heart he was also a consummate artist. His brilliance and generosity made him unique. He will be sorely missed but his memory as a kind and loving father, grandfather and friend will give comfort to his loved ones. He was preceded in death by his mother and father, Dr. Carlos F.

and Dulce Barroso, his brother, Dr. Carlos Barroso, his nephews Dr. Carlos Barroso III, Mario Barroso and Peter Bermudez. He is survived by his children Rod Barroso and Nancy Schibler (Brian Zerfas), his grandchildren Erin and Amelia, his brother Dr. Fernando Barroso, his sister Dr. Andrea Bermúdez, his best friends Dr. Ernesto and Cindy Enríquez and a host of nieces, nephews and friends.

CHAPTER 3

MY FAMILY TREE

One of the distressing consequences of life in exile has been the dispersal of family members. After many years of spatial distance, generations have grown disconnected from one another. Reunions have not been sufficient in maintaining family bonds or in establishing new ones with the relatives' offspring. Despite this reality, I have preserved some personal relations, either through powerful memories or by the good fortune of having been able to reconnect. These relations continue to fulfill a basic human need—the need to belong.

The Principals

Early in my life, I learned to love. Loving my nanny, Tata, was my first awareness that I deeply cared for someone else besides myself. She was probably the first person to ever give me more than she kept for herself. Tata joined the family as my personal caretaker. I was seven days old.

Through the years, Tata became my refuge and never left me alone. For a child, love and structure contribute to a healthy mind and body. Tata gave me both. From her, I learned to face life without fear and to accept what we have with gratitude. If I felt lonesome or misunderstood, Tata was there for me. If I was sick, she would sleep on the floor, by my side, afraid I would not make it through the night. I realize how much she must have loved me.

There are many memories of Tata sacrificing the little she had to give me the best she could. When she returned from time off to visit her family, she brought me presents, candy, and other expressions of her love and generosity. Sometimes, she would take me for visits to her family, and those times were joyful celebrations in their modest neighborhood. I felt so special, so secure. Tata's devotion to my well-being helped shape the person I am.

Tata and I at my engagement party, early summer 1960

My greatest regret is not having seen Tata again after I left for exile. The memory of her dressed up, her hair done, and anxious for being reunited but not allowed to leave the country by the authorities is much too hard to bear. I was told how she went home dejected with the realization that we would never be together again. She gave up, and not long after that, Tata was gone forever. All I had left was her memory, a fact that inspires me every day. Bittersweet memories of our love for each other are hard to revisit, as my heart has always felt heavy with grief. I know that, if there is a heaven, Tata is there, making room for me.

Father's Side: The Barrosos

I viewed my dad's side of the family as a bit aristocratic. My grandfather, Dr. Fabián Barroso, passed away long before I was born. From family pictures, I see him noble faced, tall, and handsome. According to my brother Carlos, our grandfather graduated as a medical doctor in 1888 and, a few years later, 1895, became a lieutenant colonel in the Cuban army. He went on to fight in the Independence War against Spain. After leaving the army in 1898, our grandfather went on to practice medicine in Unión de Reyes. There he met my grandmother Dulce María Piñar (Mamaquico) and her family.

My grandfather Fabián stopped practicing medicine and joined the Piñar family business, overseeing sugar production at their plantations in Babiney and La Granja. As a businessman in the sugar industry, he became the right-hand man of my great-grandfather, his father-in-law Manuel Piñar. In 1911, the family moved to Havana, and grandfather bought a new sugar mill, Central Santo Tomás, named after his father, Tomás Barroso. Eight years later, the sugar mill was sold, and the family went on an extensive trip to Europe. Their family fortune paralleled the fate of the Cuban sugar industry, and upon their return, the Depression of the 1920s was in full swing. As the sugar economy waned, so did the family wealth. In 1925, at age fifty-five, Dr. Fabián Barroso passed away, a victim of tropical anemia.

Manatí sugar mill in the eastern part of Cuba (1912-2002).
Partial view of the village (batey). My parents used to attend
military social functions while stationed in Holguín.

Grandmother Mamaquico enjoyed the trappings of old money. She had a butler welcoming you at the door, and dinner was served in style.

I still remember her enjoying the delicious chicken soup with lots of lemon and avocado chunks, while watching her favorite television program, *Liberace*. She appreciated his gift, since she was also a consummate concert pianist. As a dedicated musician, whose delicate hands covered octaves with ease and elegance, she wished to pass on her talent to her grandchildren. I remember fondly the quality time we spent together, while she taught me the basics of piano.

Although she did not succeed in making a musician out of me, she managed to pass along her love of music. I still cannot pass a piano without playing a tune she taught me over six decades ago. It always makes me smile, and in my heart, I feel I am communicating my gratitude to her. My grandparents had four children—my father Carlos, Margarita (Titahíta), Jorge (Tío Jorge), and Haydeé (Titahaydeé).

The Barroso Piñar Family
From left to right: Carlos Fabián, Margarita, Dr. Fabián
Barroso, Dulce Piñar, Jorge and Haydeé

Titahíta was a magnificent spinto soprano, and rumor has it that she was invited to join the Metropolitan Opera, but my grandfather did not think it was appropriate for any of his children to become entertainers. In preparation for singing Gounod's *Ave Maria* at my wedding, Mamaquico accompanied her during their many rehearsals. Titahíta was briefly married and had no offspring. She devoted her life to her mother and her music. She did her vocal exercises daily, and her extensive range was so powerful that the sound jolted me as a child. Critics have said that her rendition of Mimi in *La bohème* was better than professional sopranos of her time.

Titahíta was always dressed in a youthful fashion, as she was known to shave off a few years from her real age. At one point, she risked incarceration or a fine when she doctored her passport to pretend being years younger. She actually spent a few hours in detention, until the matter was clarified. Titahíta inherited the age phobia from her mother, who was well known to shear years from her actual age. My father used to say that once he had to correct her, when she gave an age five years younger than him, her oldest son! When Titahíta was well into her nineties, I took a peek at her closet, and all I saw were red dresses, a number of fancy wigs, and high-heeled black boots!

Titahaydeé was also a talented musician. Deaf at a young age, she was still able to sing and play several instruments, especially the guitar. In the early 1950s, she married a handsome Texan, Airman Herman Carmichael, and they permanently moved to the United States. They had two beautiful girls, *mis primas americanas* (my American cousins), Georgia and Diana. When my ex-husband and I left Cuba, we lived with the Carmichaels until we were able to get back on our feet. They were loving and generous, making the reality of exile less painful.

Tío Jorge was my dad's sidekick, and they both had great love and respect for each other. During the summers between 1912 and 1919, they attended Ethan Allen Military School in Vermont. According to my oldest brother, Carlos, they would get to Key West from Havana by ferry and then catch the train by themselves as early as ages twelve and eight respectively. Their love for the military never faded.

Brothers Jorge and Carlos Barroso

My uncle became a prominent sugar industrialist and political figure prior to the Castro Revolution. Tío Jorge married Virginia Palacio,
a charming woman, who helped him ride to the top echelon of Cuban
society. They had four children, Jorge Jr., Virginia, Raúl, and Ignacio. The
older boys studied law, and Jorge Jr. was running for the Senate when
Castro took over. Daughter Virginia married and moved to Spain with her
husband and four children. When her husband passed away, she moved
back to the United States permanently. Ignacio was precocious, and he
was fortunate to receive a sophisticated education in Switzerland and later
from Dartmouth College in Hanover, Massachusetts. Early in his life, he
showed signs of having inherited our grandmother's musical gene.

Tío Jorge and Tía Virginia used to rent an enormous waterfront
beach house on the spectacular Varadero beach during the summer
months. They would invite friends, as well as all their nieces and nephews. The last time I visited, the home had belonged to dictator Batista. It
was a massive pink mansion, from which you could hear the sound of the
waves and watch the dolphins come close to shore early in the morning.
I wondered then if I had died and gone to heaven.

When my uncle and his family left for exile, his house was confiscated by the Castro government. The militia locked the gate that connected with my grandmother's home, a fact that greatly distressed her.
The laughter of her children and grandchildren was replaced by the

silence of armed, bearded militia. A "No Trespassing" sign on the gate reminded my grandmother that the family was gone—and so was old Cuba. Mamaquico's mind began to fail, and soon after, she completely lost her ability to relate. Arrangements were made for her and Titahíta to leave the country. She died on January 20, 1974, in Miami, Florida.

Mother's Side: The García-Lavíns

Grandfather José Manuel was born in Guaimutas, province of Matanzas, in March 1868. He was first-generation Cuban, and during the War of Independence from Spain, he remained a Spanish sympathizer. Not so his wife, my grandmother Andrea, born in 1867, who backed the Cuban fighters against Spain. We have been told that she even hung a Cuban flag from their balcony to display her sympathies.

At the time, this was seen as an act of rebelliousness, since marriage vows of the 1890s indicated that women had to "obey" their husbands. Grandmother Andrea, a liberated thinker, passed on the gene to their five daughters, Andrea (Nena); Serafina (Fina); Gracia Irene (Niní); Julia Silvia (Julita); and my mother, Dulce María. Two boys, Ramón (Moncito) and José Manuel (Pepito) completed the García-Lavín y González family.

Mother's Parents and Siblings
From left to right: father José Manuel, brothers José Manuel and Ramón, sisters Andrea, Serafina, Gracia, mother Andrea and sister Julia

My mother's oldest living sister, my Tía Niní was another mother figure I had while growing up. Her children were young adults, so in a way, I was her first grandchild. Spoiling is a misnomer for all she and her husband did for me. When Tía Niní returned from her yearly trips to the United States, she brought me a trunk full of surprises—skirts, sweaters, dresses, penny loafers, white and brown oxfords, M&M's, toys, and anything else she thought I would like. For a child to receive all these presents was not only thrilling but also a confirmation that I was loved.

I still remember the Charlie McCarthy puppet that gave my younger brother and me many moments of fun. We built a little theater and even wrote plays that we performed for our friends and family. I also remember a puppet Tía Niní made for me to show on a children's television program. It was a Spanish señorita in a traditional flamenco dress with all its accoutrements. I may not have won first prize, but I felt my puppet deserved it. I do remember how many hours she devoted to the project. I can still see her using her Singer treadle sewing machine trying to finish my puppet on time for the performance.

She married a successful architect, Rodrigo Saavedra (Tío Tato) and had two children, Dulce María and Rodrigo, who followed in his father's footsteps. Tío Tato was known for his keen sense of humor. My brother was once telling him how impressed he was with a priest that knew 7,000 words, when most people only knew 5,000. His retort was quick. "What good is that? There are 2,000 words he can't use with anyone."

I loved spending time at their home. Tata, my three favorite dolls, and I would board the train to spend an afternoon visiting and, most especially, being spoiled. As I grew up, Tía Niní included me in her travels. When I was fourteen, I spent an academic year in Washington, DC, with her and her daughter, my godmother.

My favorite meal, fish sticks or chicken potpies, was frequently served for dinner. Tía Niní's favorite foray was visiting the soda fountain across the street after dinner and using her best English to deliver a well-rehearsed, "Good evening." One day she forgot to prepare for the salutation, and a *buenas noches* with an American accent came out instead. We got a serious case of the giggles!

Tía Niní was an extraordinary woman, and despite having had only an elementary grade education, like most women of her generation, she was well versed in classical music, opera, and baseball. Having once had a modest mezzo soprano voice, she knew all there was to know about opera. She could identify any classical piece of music by composer, movement, and opus. As for baseball, she was kind of an expert. She did not miss any of the games among our four professional teams (Habana, Almendares, Cienfuegos, and Marianao) as narrated on the radio. The sportscaster, Manolo de la Reguera, was her nephew by marriage, and he often called her to double-check statistics that she had faithfully recorded during each game.

I have great memories of Sunday double games at the Havana Stadium. Tía Niní rooted for the Almendares team, whereas her husband was a Habana fan. I was amused by their disagreements about which team was best or which would win on that day, but I had to root for hers. I was smart enough to never get involved in any of their discussions, since my culture had taught me that children's opinions had no place in adult conversation. Those memories have made me a baseball fan for life.

Tía Niní had a tough journey in exile, but her sense of humor and optimism never wavered. She was diagnosed with bone cancer, and radical surgery left her disfigured. Even the judgmental looks from people in the streets did not seem to affect her. Maybe this was a result of her strong support system led by her husband, who never stopped being her greatest fan. After his passing, she went to an assisted-living home, and she made the best out of the experience. Her only complaint was that she could not stand the "old people" at the home, bypassing the fact that she was one of them. Her cancer never returned, and she passed away peacefully at eight-five, surrounded by her children and grandchildren.

My Tía Julita was the *grande dame* of the family. Having raised seven children with husband Gastón de los Reyes, she was versed in all aspects of child rearing. When my son Peter was born in 1962, Tía Julita came every day to teach me the basics of caring for him. After his first bath, Peter looked ready for a TV ad. Her husband, Tío Gastón, was an engineer, a man of few words but of great integrity and dedication. Their children—Manolo; Silvia; twins, Gustavo and Gonzalo; Gloria; Eddy; and Lourdes—were well behaved, despite each being a strong personality. I am told that, as children, they would board the public bus, filing by in a perfect line, just like disciplined little soldiers. Sadly, Eddy passed on at five years of age of congenital heart disease.

The boys were famous for their pranks and became mentors of my eldest brother, a quick study in that department. Silvia was mostly busy with her boyfriend Ricardo, whom she married for life. Eddy looked like a blond cherub, but his frail health did not allow him to join in his brothers' mischievous activities. His untimely death weighed heavily on his parents and siblings. Gloria and Lourdes were close in age, and both had a devilish sense of humor. Their area of expertise was nicknames. A man with big, narrow feet was *"Pie de Lápiz"* (Pencil Foot); a restaurant with questionable sanitation was named thereon *"La Cuchara Sucia"* (Dirty Spoon).

I loved dining at their home. The family congregated around an enormous table and engaged in clever and animated chatter. Food preparation was exceptional, especially the black beans with olives, which made Tía Julita a favorite chef in the family. On Sundays, she prepared a mammoth tray of the most delicious ham and cheese sandwiches, enough to feed an army, including her offspring, nieces, nephews, and friends. I never wanted to miss the feast. To this day, sandwiches are my favorite meal, perhaps because of the pleasant memories they evoke.

The García-Lavín brothers Ramón (Tío Moncito) and José Manuel (Tío Pepito) were close in age and tight-knit. Tío Pepito was good-looking and built like a football player, while his older brother was not too tall, thin, and possessed the gift of gab. As children, when you saw one, the other was not too far away. As per Tío Moncito, they had made a pact that, if ever in trouble, *Tú pegas y yo hablo* ("You hit and I talk"). The brothers were feared. It was first-rate teamwork.

Tío Moncito married Aurora Fonts and fathered son José Manuel (Joche), who became an architect. Tío Pepito married Hortensia Barreto and had two children, Carlos Manuel (Forti) and José Manuel (Pastor). Forti became a psychiatrist, and his last conversation with me was to assure us that my youngest brother's diagnosis was on target and that he could function normally with proper treatment. A few weeks later, on a visit to Cuba, Forti took ill, and had to be transported back to the United States via air ambulance. He passed away shortly after.

Grandmother Andreíta with children, in-laws and grandchildren
Front row left to right: Gustavo, Gonzalo, Grandmother and Lourdes (on her lap)
Gloria, Manolo, Silvia, Carlitos, Joche, Tía Julita and Eddy
Second row left to right: Hortensia with Forti, Tío Pepito, Rodrigo, Tía
Niní, TíoTato, Mother, Father, Tío Moncito, Tía Aurora, and Tío Gastón
Missing from the picture: Cousin Dulce María Saavedra (Cuquita)

Perhaps the frequent usage of nicknames calls for clarification at this point. It was customary for a Cuban family to call relatives by another name, something that had more meaning for them. I had at least seven nicknames (La Niña, Nena, Nenita, Andreíta, Minina, Muñeca, Puchucha), depending on who was addressing me. Each was an endearing moniker, and I quickly learned to respond to whatever I was called. I do not believe that the profusion of nicknames created any confusion or identity issues for me.

Our friend Penny told me how confused she was by her partner Maria's numerous aunts called by similar names. She could not tell Cucha from Chucha or Chachi. I told her I could top her story by knowing people in my immediate family nicknamed Tato, Tata, Tito, Tuto, Toty, Tata, Titi, and Tuty and knowing exactly who each one was. We laughed and realized how cultural differences can explain so much of who we are and how we behave.

I am also reminded of our friend Chiquitico ("Little One"), a nickname earned because he was the youngest of his siblings. We knew him as a robust fifty-something practicing psychiatrist, who still answered to his nickname. It took me a few days to recall his given name, Dr. Leoncio A. García, MD, aka Chiquitico.

My First Friends: Toty, Pablito, and Pet Lady

Toty

Toty (Margarita Herrera) was my first friend. Toty was born a month before me, and she and I were inseparable. She was blond, blue-eyed, and tall. I was her counterpoint, with my jet-black hair, brown eyes, and short stature. We attended the same elementary school and shared our Catholic milestones together. We even took each other's name at confirmation.

Toti (left) and I dressed up for carnival circa 1945

On weekends we would go to a sugar mill in Matanzas, Central Limones, which her dad, Benito, administered. The Herrera family was provided a big hacienda as living quarters and lots of acres to enjoy horseback riding and eating tropical fruits directly from their luxuriant trees, including *mamoncillo* (Spanish lime), a forbidden fruit because of its dangerous seed that, if swallowed, would cause choking.

We also attended the one and only movie theater in the town, a small room furnished with uncomfortable church pews, which showed old cowboy movies. A favorite was Johnny Mack Brown, known by the locals as Johnny Mambró, a well-known American movie star of the 1940s and 1950s. It was fun to hear the comments of the audience; many could not read the Spanish subtitles and made up an original storyline instead.

A typical celebration in Central Limones was the roasted pig, which took twenty-four hours to cook. We frequently checked on its progress, tasting an occasional sliver. It was a ritual for holidays, and we loved every minute of it. Another event we enjoyed was riding on the sugarcane trolley that traveled on the train tracks. These were magical weekends for young kids, and I cherish those memories.

Toty's dad had been the chief of police of Havana during our early years in elementary school, and we were driven to school in a *perseguidora* (police car). I am sure we felt important, and our classmates were probably green with envy!

High school took Toty and me in different directions. So as teenagers, we moved in different circles.

After leaving Cuba in 1960, I had seen Toty only twice. I could hardly remember that first visit if it were not for a photograph. She called me when my Peter died in 1982, but after that, we lost contact with each other for a long time. On a recent visit to Florida, I decided that fifty plus years not seeing my friend was too long and researched her contact information. It was meant to be when I instantaneously found a valid phone number and an address. I picked up the phone and called. It was so pleasant to hear her voice after so many years. We agreed on a visit three days later, as we both knew that, at our age, postponing something was an iffy proposition. She made me laugh when she said, "We better have a *cartelito*" (sign) with our names in order to recognize each other.

Suddenly, fear invaded me. I had never been afraid to move forward and face the music. But the past was different. Our memories involved loss. I was not sure that I was ready to revisit my childhood, when feelings about the world are so innocent and worries about our destiny nonexistent.

The day of the visit arrived, and I was still not sure if this reconnection was going to bring back whatever emotions I had buried deeply in my subconscious. As I drove through the upscale neighborhood of Toty's home, I was invaded by a feeling of insecurity.

It all went away when my childhood friend opened the door to her lovely place. Warmth and love replaced my fear. She looked terrific. I told her I would have recognized her after so many years. I also told her how glad I was of this fact, since we were each other's mirrors, having been born only a month apart. She thought I had also fought my battles without any visible scars.

We talked for three and a half hours. She showed me pictures of our childhood. I was invariably in almost every one of them. We talked about great times in Limones and our fun visits to "El Castillito," a small castle designed on a steep hill on the Matanzas Bay by her renowned architect grandfather Félix Cabarrocas.

Toty had visited Cuba three years earlier. The Castillito was still there, and her pictures evoked joyful memories. Limones was another story. The sugar mill was gone, and so was the big hacienda we'd so much enjoyed. That did not stop us from reconstructing the village as we fondly remembered it.

We laughed, and we chatted with pleasure about our childhood adventures. Two grandmothers were now joyfully reliving memories of years gone by. As I departed, we promised that, this time, reconnection would last. I had always yearned for validation of people and events I remembered, but there was no one there to tell me if they had actually happened or if I had made them up. Visiting with Toty and reconstructing our past met that yearning.

My previous misgivings about reliving past experiences were replaced by a more complete acceptance of my own destiny and the realization that the past is mostly lessons and memories. Closing its door without facing what our experiences mean will only serve to extend our sense of loss, rather than helping us accept the past as a tool to enhance our present journey.

Pablito

At age twelve, I fell in love with a thirteen-year-old boy named Pablito González Menocal. My parents had been invited to a party across the street, and Pablito had shown up with his mom and dad. Having sought my parents' approval, the hosts decided to give me a call to see if I wanted to join the party. As we say in Spanish, "Do you ask a fish if it wants water?" I was there in record time. It was love at first sight. For the first time, I danced in public and visited with a boy while being chaperoned by over fifty adults, including our parents.

The next few years were memorable. Both sets of parents were delighted with the young romance, and many fun times followed. I particularly remember Pablito's equestrian competitions, where he introduced me to the rich and famous, one of them being President Batista's son Jorge. I have a clear memory of how my school bus had to pass by Pablito's house, and I can still feel the excitement of waving at this handsome boy in his blue La Salle school uniform. What he never knew was that I was sitting on top of my textbooks to look taller! The love interest was short-lived, as most young love is, but it left me a sweet memory of my early teens.

The beauty of early love is that, by definition, it is genuine, truly personal, and not shaped by external forces. As we age, there is a tendency to fit people and feelings into terms and definitions enhanced by media, created by others. Celebratory events such as engagements, weddings, and honeymoons can, in reality, encourage feelings that may not be there. Being in love with love is hardly the same as being in love.

Pet Lady

My siblings and I grew up sharing a love for animals. Our first pet was Lady D'Irack, a pointer of champion lines, who loved leftovers and became sort of an escape artist. She taught me tenderness when I saw her caring for her seven puppies.

I also learned that you cannot get away with murder. On one occasion, my mother was planning a party and borrowed a beautiful centerpiece, a dove, from my grandmother. Before the guests arrived, she noticed there were feathers everywhere, and only few other remnants of the borrowed centerpiece. It all pointed to Lady, the hunter, who was trying to conceal her guilt with little success.

I do not remember the punishment, which I am sure was not great, since Lady enjoyed a very high status in the pecking order. Whatever the penalty was, it worked well enough that she did not try her hunting skills indoors again. Along with Lady, we had our menagerie of cats, a parrot, a monkey, turtles, and parakeets. My parents believed that children become more caring adults when raised with animals. Fortunately, this lesson was passed along to the next generations.

Loss of Biological Family Bond

The most devastating consequence of the Communist takeover in Cuba was the decimation of the family unit. For those who stayed, children belonged to the state. The traditional family responsibility of handing down value systems and beliefs to the next generation was taken away. For those of us who left, it was not ideology that separated us but vast geographical distances that managed to diminish our family connections.

Family members dispersed through Puerto Rico, Spain, and at least eight states in the United States. My own immediate family represented Texas, Maryland, Virginia, Florida, and Georgia. What seemed amusing when my parents heard their grandchildren exhibit the various regional "accents" was actually a symbol of a tragic loss. The children grew up in different worlds, as strangers to one another. We had to redefine family to refer to the amazing friendships that we have made along the way. And although feeling privileged, we grieve the loss of our biological family.

CHAPTER 4

DNA PLUS: NATURAL AND ACQUIRED TRAITS

I am inspired by the work of Spanish philosopher José Ortega y Gasset, who defined the self as a melding of the individual with the surrounding environment. *Yo soy yo y mi circunstancia* (I am I and my circumstance) summarizes his belief that we cannot ignore the external influences that, along with the ego, define the totality of the person. Similarly, I view myself as an aggregate of my inherited DNA and the valuable lessons life has taught me.

Family Traits

Smarts run in my family on both sides. My father and his brother Jorge were exceptional children, whose solid intellect showed early. In a way, they would do what most kids do—play. What was different in their games was that they reenacted historic wars with their toy soldiers, in minute detail. For little boys to have studied intensively those histories was an indication of their formidable intelligence and curiosity. My dad became a physician, who specialized in diseases of the lung. He saved many lives at a time when a cure for tuberculosis was still a remote possibility.

My father maintained his love and knowledge of military history throughout his life. I always remember him surrounded by his extensive library, which I was convinced he had committed to memory. One of his favorite games was to ask us to draw a squiggly, which, in under a minute, he would convert into a cavalry officer, mustache and all! I still laugh remembering the Merthiolate tattoos he would draw on our arms or legs after giving us a shot. Mother was not amused, but we were.

Father's brother Jorge became a lawyer, a senator, and a department secretary during the Batista regime. He also served as president of the Cuban Institute for the Stabilization of Sugar, the regulatory agency that set sugar quotas. Tío Jorge was considered the brainpower of the sugar industry of the time.

On Mother's side, smarts showed in an earthier way. Mother and her family were the wise ones not as cerebral in their approach to life, but equally successful in figuring out how to navigate the real world and its challenges. Tío Tato was perhaps the exception, as he obtained degrees in architecture and civil engineering and a doctorate in physics and mathematics. As a typical genius, he was quite absentminded. Once, after buying a brand-new car and forgetting about it, he arrived home by train. Needless to say, my tía made him go back, and bring the new car home. Tío Tato was a Renaissance man. He could compose poetry, discuss philosophy, or solve a difficult calculus problem.

Tío Tato's passport picture, circa 1960

My mother, on the other hand, would have agreed with the late French historian, Hippolyte Taine, who said, "I have studied many philosophers and cats. The wisdom of cats is infinitely superior." That was my mother's kind of smart—being astute and pragmatic. She may not have liked calculus much, but she could solve any difficult life problem without effort. She was also a strong believer in the power of education. For a woman of the early 1900s, it is remarkable that she was able to overcome conventional obstacles and obtain advanced educational credentials.

Being genuine is another trait that runs in the family. With few exceptions, it is hard to find any relatives who were not true to self or who pretended to be something they were not. My mother's sister, Tía Niní, believed Cuban politics were so corrupt that voting, although required by law, was not worth the effort. Her refusal finally got her into police custody. Sitting in the back of a *perseguidora,* she was unbending. My poor uncle had to figure out how make use of his connections to release her. He was embarrassed. She felt vindicated!

Loving all forms of life defines most of my family members. As stated in an earlier chapter, pets were as pampered as kids, a trait that has been inherited by the next generation.

Granddaughter Kat and her buddy Samson, 2013

My daughters Flori and Julie are convinced that the secret is out, and they find cats and dogs dropped at their doorstep. On our way to the Dallas Love Field for my return from a visit, Julie spotted a duck that seemed to have been hurt by traffic. Before I could react, we were making a U-turn on busy Josey Lane to pick it up. Granddaughter Julianne covered the duck with a towel, and held it with her right hand, while she left-handedly researched on her phone the location of the Dallas wildlife rescue. The lucky duck was taken there right after they dropped me off. It had injured one of its wings, but the veterinarian promised full recovery. The clan was thrilled.

Dogs, cats, turtles, lizards, mice, birds, and fish are my grandpets. Recently, granddaughter Julianne's dog, Lassie, was nearing the end of her days. The children would take turns sleeping with Lassie, so she would not be scared and alone. A month after her death, my son found a note from Andrea, eight. It read:

> I know it is hard to let go of Lassie, but someday you will be cuddling her in heaven.
>
> Love, Andrea.

Humorous Relatives

My family is well endowed with characters with funny bones. Both of my parents were well known for their sense of humor. For my dad, it was his philosophy of life, his best medicine, and the lens through which he looked at life. As the story was told, Father had been asked to say a few words at an award ceremony for a fellow physician. He was a bit apprehensive, wanting to do a good job for his friend. As he prepared to introduce the *homenajeado* (honoree), he got tongue twisted and called him *homojado.* He kept trying to fix his mistake on the spot (*menejeado, mojoneado, mojonudo*), but the more he tried, the closer it sounded to the word *mojón* (turd). By then, he had lost the audience to laughter and was never able to live down calling the honoree, his good friend, a turd.

Peter and Abuelo making us laugh, circa 1966

Mother was frequently at the center of hilarious episodes. An everyday experience would become a funny anecdote. Picture the following: A night at the movies. Mother and Father are comfortably seated in the theater. She is sporting a beautiful chignon and looks radiant, as always. Behind them, a bulky man in a white tropical suit is walking past them, and she feels her jet-black hairpiece jostled.

She looks back, and her hairpiece is attached to the man's zipper! What followed needs no description!

Although not necessarily a baseball fan, she loved to attend games at the stadium on occasional Sundays. Unlike real fans, she would dress to the hilt, as always sporting her freshwater white pearls *à la* Barbara Bush. At some point, a great catch made us all stand up and cheer, while the two men next to Mother were arguing at full volume. Suddenly, one turns to her saying, "Lady, if Havana runs out of shit, this man will starve." Mother's quick wit evaded her this time, and she remained uncommonly wordless.

Another time, while watching a sad movie at the theater, she cried and cried, which made blowing her nose a necessity. When the movie ended, Mother proceeded to return her hanky to her purse, while moving towards the aisle. At the same time, someone sitting next to her was saying, "Excuse me, you caught part of my dress in your purse." I cannot describe mother's embarrassment, albeit a moment for posterity, when she realized that the entire time she had been using her neighbor's dress instead of her handkerchief! Mother was humorous, but paradoxically, she looked at life fearing the worst would happen.

My father was the reverse. Life was full of humor, and he was always looking for an angle to create optimism. When he was in his nineties, he received a call from an insurance company trying to sell him life insurance. He had fun setting up the salesman with his keen interest in offering a low-cost package to help my dad build a nest egg. After a while, the salesman came around to asking Dad how old he was, and the answer left him speechless. My father, in his usual casual style, broke the silence by saying, "Why are you shocked? Am I supposed to be dead?" Seeing humor in all facets of life served him well in extending his journey beyond his hundredth birthday.

Uncle Tato usually accompanied wife Niní on her frequent trips to the United States. Although his English-speaking skills were modest, at best, he always volunteered as a translator. On one of their explorations, there was a much-needed word missing from their vocabulary, as they wanted to visit a wax museum. He assured Aunt Niní that he could ask a lady sitting on a park bench leisurely reading the newspaper. Looking for the word "wax," he approached her, probably sitting too close.

With hands flying in the air, he asked in his best broken English, "Lady, the bee produces two things. One is the honey, and the other is ..."

To his chagrin, the lady did not fill in the blank. Instead, she left hurriedly, looking back to see if the weird stranger was following.

Mother's older brother, Tío Moncito, has kept us in stitches with his creative theories and interpretations of the world around him. Sitcoms were his specialty. Since he was hard of hearing, his particular take of what was happening was sometimes much better than the actual show. One, in particular, he thought was an absolute bore. The program was set on the high seas with submarines as primary goings-on. Tío would say, "I can't believe people watch other people being tossed side to side for a whole hour." Of course, he would underscore his words by a highly amusing demonstration.

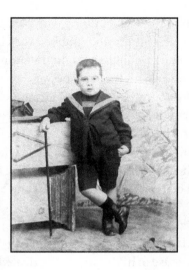

Tío Moncito in 1903

Much like his siblings, he could find humor in most anything. One day my mother asked him to entertain a neighbor for a few minutes while she ran errands. To mother's surprise, the neighbor was gone when she returned, so she asked him what had happened. Our partially deaf Tío responded, "Oh, it went well. She sat down, talked to herself for a few minutes, and then left."

Also on mother's side, her sister Julita was strong, independent, and had a wicked sense of humor. Her husband, Gastón, was an engineer whose definite views of the world befitted his profession. When they were a young married couple in the late 1910s, Tío Gastón felt it was inappropriate for his wife to leave home every afternoon to visit friends and relatives. According to family legend, he put a lock on her armoire so she could not access her clothing. It is rumored that, with the aid of a hatchet, she tore the lock to pieces. She went on with her errands. He never mentioned the incident again.

Tata, my beloved caretaker, was also a comic, despite the fact that she had a serious persona most of the time. She loved to chew tobacco, and her favorites were my dad's leftover Havana cigars. One day, Dad was delighting in his smoke, when he noticed Tata following him. Right away, he knew what she was keeping an eye on, so he decided to give her a hard time. He walked around the house puffing with pleasure with Tata in tow. She could not stand it any longer and grabbed the cigar from his mouth saying, "*Basta ya*" (Enough)! Tata could do no wrong, so we all thought the incident was hysterical, and the story became a part of the family lore.

As a little boy, my youngest brother Rod was active and a bit on the rowdy side. No matter how filthy he got, he was still a fashionista, always wearing his favorite ring and one of our father's ties. One day, I heard our mother blaming Rod, then five years of age, for leaving dirty palm prints on the wall. I heard her say, "Rod, I can see your five fingers on the wall!"

He responded in defiance. "Sure, as if I were the only one in the house with five fingers."

Of course, the size of the "five fingers" gave him away.

A couple of years later, the older cousins enjoyed asking Rod why he had to wear eyeglasses because of his highly sophisticated response—"*Tengo*" (I have)"*astigmatismo hipermetrópico e hipermetropía*"—a mouthful for a seven-year old!

Rod riding my beloved red and blue wooden scooter, circa 1945

There are funny bones in the next generation as well. My son Peter not only had a twinkle in his eye, he also sported a devilish wittiness. While I was on a trip, my friend Margaret offered to take care of the children who were between the ages of twelve to fourteen. E. J. volunteered to sleep in the room addition by the pool, while Margaret was staying in my room. He thought it would be easier to "escape" without Margaret knowing and join his friend Brett for some mischief. So he sneaked out as planned, returning home about 11:00 p.m.

There was a note on his bed. "See me when you get home. Margaret."

Contrite and scared, E. J. knocked on her door, waking her up, while saying, "Sorry, Margaret. I will never do this again," only to find out Peter had written the note.

My seven-year old grandson, Max, is considered our next generation funny man. Born to clown, he would entertain us as a baby with funny faces and noises that made us laugh. Once he could walk, he loved to shadow dance to his ballerina older sister, taking away the center of attention. Now, as an articulate young man, his sayings are known as "Maxisms" to the family. When he was about five, he and his mom had the following exchange:

Max. "Mama, can I have a snack?"

Julie. "You just had breakfast."

Max. "That's not a snack!

One of Max's inimitable expressions

On another occasion, at about the same age, Max asked me, "Nani, why do you call me 'sugar'?"

My response was the obvious. "Because you are sweet."

He pondered my words for a while, followed by, "Ah!"

A bit later, he overheard me calling his sister "sugar," to which he retorted, "She is *not* sugar. I *am* sugar."

Having a humorous family is such a gift! Their stories continue to help us go through life with a more positive frame of mind. It is also a reminder that you are part of that genetic history. I have many times been saved by seeing humor in whatever experience I have had to face.

My Way or the Highway

On the negative side, most family members adhered to very strict principles shaped by their Catholicism. Codes of behavior were not to be challenged, and as a result, some of us became the part we were expected to play. Since the value system of the Cuban culture before Castro was strongly fashioned by the church, it tended to create, and feed, the gender double standard we discussed earlier. Men had more "wiggle room" in what was expected from them, and they could usually do as they pleased, while women's behavior reflected the family's honor and place in society. It was commonplace to give more value to a man's opinion, or expect that women would not challenge men's views publicly on most subjects. Although there were no written rules, members of both genders understood their place, and if anyone dared to challenge this dictum, the person was "wrong" by default.

I spent most of my adult life in the closet. I ran away from those, including family, who I felt would be judgmental. I viewed the family as intolerant, even bigoted, since my older brothers made it clear they regarded my lifestyle unfavorably. I may have missed some family members who might have been accepting, but I could not afford emotionally to be rejected. It was clear to me that their actions and opinions were not intentionally hurtful. I saw them as victims of their own socialization. I was fortunate in that I could separate myself from the expectations of others and build my own self-image based on how I viewed myself in this life, what I had accomplished, and what I intended to accomplish in the future.

A happy event happened in fall 2016, when I reconnected with the next generation at a family reunion gathered at the Vermont vacation home of one of Tia Julita's grandchildren, Gastón de los Reyes. I was, on average, ten years older than my second cousins, but from the get-go, we were connected not only by blood, but also by the loving acceptance and respect we felt for one another. Our pasts were our common link, but the future as kindred was definitely assured.

We reminisced about our departed parents and grandparents. We laughed with gusto at stories shared. We spoke earnestly about our homes, our childhoods, our upbringing, and our challenges. One night, with the stars shining brightly in the clear skies of New England, we rested on cushions and gazed at the breathtaking panorama. We shared humorous stories and laughed so hard that we woke up the rest of the household. We were one, held together by our appreciation of each other and in celebration of having become a family again.

Nature and Nurture: How I See Myself

Just like everyone else, I am the product of my genetic history as it intermingles with the experiences my journey has provided. Among many traits, I inherited attitude from my father and personality type and some physical characteristics from my mother. Life lessons have provided much of the rest.

There are many things I like about myself. These are mostly gifts that came with birth. Some I cultivate, but others are just "there" without any need to intervene other than the rewards received as a result. Appreciating humor, for instance, is not a learned trait. It is just how one views everything in life. If we are always looking for the amusing side of events or value "funny" in others, we have the gift. At times, the "funny" will come from you, and it becomes reinforced when others laugh. No matter which definition I use, I know I was born appreciating the role of humor in my life.

From my father, I inherited an optimistic lens. I put it to a test not too long ago. Everyone who knows me is aware that air travel is not one of my favorite doings, especially when I think about a few near misses I have experienced. On a trip back home to Houston, the captain announced trouble with the landing gears. The copilot had been in and out of the cabin, checking for something on the floorboards.

An announcement that the flight would go directly to Houston, rather than an anticipated stop in New Orleans, made me a bit anxious. I asked the young man sitting next to me where the emergency door was located, and his answer was, "You are sitting on it." That made me realize I was even more apprehensive than I'd thought. For whatever reasons, I was able to practice a crash-landing, along with the rest of the passengers without a panic attack. The flight attendant asked us to remove our jewelry and place our heads on our laps, as soon as we were within landing range. While removing my jewelry, I decided that, just in case our landing was successful, I would stick a ten-dollar bill in my jeans' back pocket for happy hour.

The saga had a fortunate ending. Landing gear had been stuck in the ready position, so we landed without further drama. I also found out something important about myself during the serious emergency. I never lost my faith on a happy ending to our dilemma, relying on my dad's example of always trying to find a positive angle in whatever he had to face.

The Power of Role Models

For some people, giving is more of a blessing than receiving. Or as Kahlil Gibran said in *Sand and Foam*, "Generosity is not in giving me that which I need more than you do, but it is in giving me that which you need more than I do." Many mentors have taught me by example this art of giving. I always think of my childhood caretaker, Tata, who had very little but gave it all away to others. As the center of her universe, I was showered with her love, gifts, and care. Her example is so vivid that every time an opportunity to give presents itself, I feel her presence encouraging me: "Just do it!"

My partner is another role model in the "giving department." Aside from her many commitments to charity and environmental causes, she is constantly giving of herself. I am always amused when I think of the time she came across a $100 bill on the floor of a casino and was getting ready to turn it in to security. I could picture the whole casino claiming *their* "loss."

Both Tata and Deb have taught me the joy giving, but I still need to learn to feel comfortable accepting the largesse of others.

Deb enjoying Pueblo Blanco, NM in 2010

Life as a Teacher

Early on, I learned the power of being organized. Goal setting, planning, and executing principles not only guided my daily life; they ruled it. I found them helpful in achieving results, although at times they kept me from savoring the present. I have learned with the passing of time that issues have a way of resolving themselves with minimal intrusion. I had always thought of myself as a problem solver, which created the need to take multiple notes, to research the issues involved, and to create best-case and worst-case scenarios to prepare a response. I know now that a little less of those activities does not seem to harm the outcome.

Solutions are a good thing, as long as we don't rush past the present moment to attain them. Agreeing with my brother Rod's words, "Today is the yesterday of tomorrow," I try to seize the moment before it is gone forever. Being a survivor is not necessarily the direct result of one's accomplishments. It has more to do with appreciating the present for what it is and finding what part we should be playing.

I have always dreaded unfinished business, although because of having to raise three children, I became a multitasker with a large number of "balls in the air." The need for closure and the feeling that having to do more than one thing at a time are mutually exclusive and a recipe for potential disaster. The need for closure, when taken to an extreme, becomes obsessive, even if one is dealing with a hobby or a distraction. I have been victim of "decorating" during my waking hours in the middle of the night, until I realized that a good night's sleep would feed better ideas in the morning! On the other hand, I have to admit that I have been able to accomplish my education because of my need for closure, coupled with the ability to multitask. Both are valuable traits, but I learned that competing needs have to be managed, or else we become their victim. The secret to everything in life is balance.

When I wrote *The Incomplete Traveler*, my earlier book about the Cuba I left, I was totally obsessed with its completion. I wrote for eight hours every day; brought my computer and voice recorder everywhere; and, in general, made a chore out of an otherwise pleasurable undertaking. The experience taught me to approach writing my memoir differently. Not afraid to forget any ideas, I have learned the importance of setting the project aside for the next day and taking a real break from time to time. In doing so, I was following the advice of famous writer Ernest Hemingway, who advised writers, "Don't think about your writing when you are not writing." The master's suggestion has boosted my enjoyment of the process, and prevented me from becoming obsessive-compulsive about my projects.

Insidious Cultural Brainwashing

In our journey, we encounter challenges that only become obstacles if we pay attention to the barrage of messages coming our way from different directions. Age, weight, and external beauty are three man-made obsessions that we tend to elevate to the realm of personal problems.

Aging, for instance, is a gift, a privilege that some people never experience. The choice would be not aging, which is hardly a smart solution. Weight and external beauty are also cultural obsessions exacerbated by the influence of media, which set the parameters for what is acceptable. The ultraslim, tall, blond is more frequent in James Bond's movies than in real life. Beauty contests, movies, product advertisements, and television programs promote a definition of beauty that is not necessarily attained by most people.

Especially in youth, this type of campaign sets off serious problems, such as anorexia nervosa, an often-fatal condition that makes the victim stop eating in order to lose weight. We need to look at weight as a matter of health, and not as a synonym for beauty. If we design a plan that fits our lifestyle, we improve the quality of our day-to-day living. This is definitely easier said than done, as we must also find a way to see ourselves in a positive light despite the noise around us.

A recent Facebook posting caught my eye: "Warning: Reflections in this mirror may be distorted by socially constructed ideas of *beauty*" (Single Dad Laughing, June 2016). If when I look at the mirror, I see an old, unbecoming person looking back, I am fighting a lost battle. If, instead, I see a warrior, a survivor who has somehow managed to continue the journey in good spirits, I cannot help but admire what I see and think of ways to support this warrior.

When my mother was younger than I am now, someone gave her a makeup mirror as a present. One side was magnified. She looked at herself with dismay, adding "Who in their right mind would give a mirror to a maturing woman?"

Sadly, she was not seeing the same person I was looking at—a beautiful, strong survivor whose life made a difference to so many. I always remember this exchange and tell myself, When you look at a mirror, look for the warrior. She is there, stronger and wiser than ever!

Accepting what can't be changed and recognizing the insignificance of these cultural obsessions are must-learn lessons. Doing so calls for disavowing public opinion and discovering for ourselves how each of our challenges can best be addressed. There are good and bad lessons we receive as we go through life. Sometimes it's hard to distinguish between them, as many of the destructive messages are subliminal in nature. We are not always aware of the lessons learned, so we must develop a sixth sense to become selective as to which lessons would serve us best in life.

PART II

MY UPBRINGING

CHAPTER 5

GROWING UP CUBAN

I was born in a sexist culture. I have argued previously that the patterns of behavior traditionally recognized in pre-Castro Cuba were modeled after the Catholic hierarchy. The history of the church demonstrates a male-dominated structure with ultimate decisions left to popes, cardinals, bishops and priests, while nuns occupy positions of service. The world of the spirit is also portrayed by a male Trinity, including a God and his son. It is difficult to escape the blatant message that males top the hierarchy and, by design, are the ones with the qualities to lead and decide. This two-tiered model was superimposed on the Cuban culture of my time, opening opportunities for advancement mostly to men. For centuries, men were expected to assume decision-making roles, while women were relegated to domestic responsibilities.

Growing Up in a Sexist Environment

Life with three brothers cemented the message. Rules were different for them than for me. I was protected, escorted by chaperons who made sure that I would be home safe, sound, and early. The boys were less restricted, since they did not have the responsibility I had of representing the family name. My brothers were free to roam and to have girlfriends of their choice. I could only befriend or date boys who carried the family approval.

I was never by myself, always in the company of a vigilant adult.

Despite the double standard, my mother defied essential aspects of the culture, such as education and career, and she made sure that my brothers and I received the same educational opportunities. I accepted the double standard as my destiny and knew there would be no David or Goliath who could change it.

Cultural Expectations for Females

Born only eight years after women were allowed to vote in Cuba, I was destined to live in the shadow of a father or a husband. Since women were obligated to strictly follow the dictates of the church, the domestic role of a wife and mother was the cultural ideal. In those days, there were two kinds of women—the marriageable ones and those who, due to their liberated ways, were considered outcasts. Prostitutes and mistresses were pariahs, although they obviously needed male collaboration to get there.

Unwanted pregnancies were the woman's shame and lifelong responsibility. Men escaped judgment unscathed, as womanizing was seen as an attribute to their masculinity. The choice of being an "old maid" had no social advantage, as guardianship was still the responsibility of a male figure, the father or an older brother. From the father's home to the husband's was the expected trajectory of a woman's life.

Although the possibility of a career was available, the majority of women pursued service professions, either teaching or nursing. Despite social restrictions, a small number of women managed a balance between domesticity and a career. As I have said before, my mother challenged the established mores, by attaining a university degree and pursuing a career outside the home, although still within the constraints of a service profession.

Machismo, defined as male domination, helped craft the double standard for gender expectations. Adultery, for example, was penalized in women, while accepted in men. Should separation or divorce follow, women would not be eligible to receive child support. Men were free to engage in illicit relationships, but women were expected to maintain the integrity of the family name by never deviating from their marriage vows. Childbearing and child rearing were entirely the responsibility of women, while maintaining a subordinate role outside the home.

During the Castro revolution, however, women took a more active public function. Many female rebels fought side by side with their male counterparts, but the gender disparity did not totally disappear.

My relationship to the church also became affected as I finally saw myself as a victim of cultural abuse. I viewed the hierarchy for what it was—a way to keep women under wraps, while men decided what was to be. Until the 1960s, nuns wore habits that barely showed their faces, and definitely hid any part of their bodies that hinted at their being female.

Nuns were not only considered second-class citizens, but also acted as mere servants, while priests played centers of the universe. Dressed for Mass in elaborate attire, priests looked more like peacocks seeking attention than men of the cloth. These were powerful visuals that suggested to me that I had been deceived.

Parental Expectations of a Daughter

My parents supported my plans to get married and have children, so I would fulfill the culturally accepted role of a Cuban woman of my generation. Domesticity was considered not only desirable but also almost a mandatory feminine trait. I clearly remember my dad's embarrassment over the fact that, in preparation for marriage, I had not learned how to cook. Disregard the fact that my husband to be did not know how to cook either, but that skill was not expected of him.

When I became a professional, my dad, for instance, did not know what I did or where I worked, as for him, my real accomplishments were of a personal nature. In his eyes, being mother to Peter, Flori, and E.J. was a most significant achievement, which I did not have to exceed. When I received a promotion to associate provost at the university, I wanted to share my pride with my dad, but I found instead an unimpressed reaction. Actually, he said something like, "Good, and your brother was named chair of his department." To him, I did not have to achieve anything beyond motherhood, while my brother, as a man, was the one expected to have professional accomplishments.

Having so much emphasis on marriage and motherhood, one can imagine the devastation a divorce would cause in such an ultraconventional environment. News of my impending divorce rocked the family. Mother first reacted by crying uncontrollably, and Father, obviously upset, indicated his utter disapproval. For them, divorce was not a solution to an unhappy marriage; it was a sign of moral decay. My job then was to convince them otherwise. My feelings of freedom the day I made the announcement to both our families contrasted with their low-spirited reaction. I felt, for the first time, that a future was possible, but it would only happen if I went at it alone.

I explained to my parents that I had goals in my life for my family and for myself and that I could no longer be lost in my husband's destiny. It did not take them long to realize that I was taking responsibility for my life. And from then on, both parents became my greatest supporters. From buying furniture for our home to taking the children on an extensive trip to Europe, my parents were there for us. I realize how much of the initial reaction had been the habitual influence of our native culture. What was amazing to me was seeing them embrace change and move on with the times.

Sexism in Marriage

I married into a very well-respected, traditionalist Catholic family that exemplified the notion of female subservience. My husband's parents firmly believed that a couple's spiritual salvation depended on the wife's onus to pray for both and remain virtuous. My husband to be was the youngest of five. He grew up pampered, believing that he was the center of the universe. His mother, an old-fashioned "woman behind the man," was convinced her boys were deserving of the best life had to offer, as they were gifts to this world. There were four boys and one girl in a family committed to having at least a couple of children devoted to the church. The girl became a nun, and my ex-husband was destined for the priesthood. After several years of theological training, Pedro Pablo decided that the ministry was not his calling.

When I married, I became Andrea Barroso de Bermúdez. Common

language usage uncovers evidence of a culture's social norms and attitudes. In Spanish, the preposition "de" (of, belongs to) is used to designate a woman's surname after marriage, while the husband's remains unchanged. So, in essence, on my wedding day, I became my husband's property. It is customary to refer to the wife as *mi mujer* (my woman), a use not applied to the husband (*mi esposo, mi marido*). Additionally, their progeny takes on the husband's last name. I have had a hard time trying to locate female classmates, as their family's surnames have been replaced. It gave me an eerie feeling that my friends had ceased to exist after marriage.

My former husband's family supported the double standard. I remember a conversation with my mother-in-law after I had successfully completed a master's degree, urging me to stay home and take care of my domestic obligations. I could not help myself in responding that I had not sacrificed that long for her son alone, but for the future of our children. She never understood my determination to continue my schooling, as, in her opinion, the domestic role (*ama de casa*) I should have assumed did not require any.

The Bermúdez clan in Lynchburg, Virginia, 1967

Childhood Dreams and Sexism

As a child, I dreamed of becoming an architect. I felt it was so awesome to design a home that would also make a unique artistic statement. My uncle Tato and his talented son had an architectural firm, and would bring me to their office to let me pretend I worked there. I would sit at the drawing table, feet dangling, awkwardly handling a T-ruler, and spend hours sketching my own house plans. I remember my cousin, who was an accomplished architect, encouraging me as he looked at what I had drafted. He would sometimes softly point to the fact that adding a door or two would help people move from one room to another, a very diplomatic way of telling me I had excluded doors in my design!

In fall 1958, I managed to complete a first semester in architecture at the University of Villanova before Castro came to power and closed the institution. My dream was further detoured when I became engaged to be married. Since architecture was mostly a male world, it was more appropriate for a woman about to be married to move instead to a service career. Teaching became my new major.

Sometimes before a dream can become a blueprint, fate changes its course, and an unexpected experience takes place. I would have loved to become an accomplished architect. But, obviously, fate got in my way. It is almost like life replaces your dream without asking you first. That is how I feel that my profession as a university professor, writer of textbooks, and later academic administrator happened.

Despite the abrupt change of direction, I have never forgotten my love for architecture, and I find myself planning and designing homes, which mostly stay in the realm of a dream. Having said this, I have no regrets for having followed the path of university professor, as it has brought many personal rewards. Most importantly, I have seen many of my former students moving forward in their professional lives as teachers, also making a difference in the lives of others. Being honored by former students with the Starfish Award, in recognition of my contributions, was a most meaningful tribute. It reinforced that my professional journey had been fruitful and that it would continue through others after its conclusion.

Defying Sexism

Despite the fact that early efforts to fight gender inequality were made in Cuba, nothing much changed through the years. Cuban feminists found their voice in a 1918 journal, and the *avant-garde* 1940 Constitution of Cuba made promises on equality by prohibiting sex discrimination and supporting equal pay for equal work. Despite these efforts, society remained patriarchal and authoritative, allowing for the chasm between genders to prevail.

Since expectations about my place as a woman in society were preordained, I never thought beyond becoming "the woman behind the man." It is a wonder that any woman would defy such cultural pressures, but I consider my mother one example of defiance that has been my lifelong inspiration. To her, education was the most expedient way to attain a more functional role in the family's decision-making. Serving as a role model for us, she instilled in each of her children the desire for educational advancement. When she died, her obituary listed her children and husband with a "Dr." preceding each name.

Another female role model for me was a well-known Cuban architect, Gabriela Menéndez, who managed to succeed in a male-dominated profession. Menéndez was credited with helping bring about modernism to Cuban architecture and left her mark in buildings of great beauty, such as Ciudad Deportiva, Teatro Nacional, the Havana Hilton, and Riviera hotels. In general, women's contributions were played down, which discouraged the young from following in the footsteps of successful professional women.

Sexism of a Different Sort

With minimal "survival" tools, I started my married life in the United States. I immediately observed a significant difference with American women. I saw them as more confident, independent, and whole. It was pleasing to see husbands helping wives in the care of their children and couples working side by side in their marriages. That was quite a contrast with my home life, where I was in full charge of the domestic duties of the marriage, while my husband had the responsibility of providing. Even in church, I looked like a Christmas tree with my children affixed as ornaments, while he prayed, unattached.

I also observed that, in the United States, the gender double standard was more understated, although the past history of female subordination was similar in both countries. American women won voting rights in 1920, but it was not until recently that they were allowed to participate in battle.

In earlier history, women fought wars disguised as men. And if discovered, they would either suffer punishment or be honorably discharged. In 1782, Deborah Sampson was one of these women. Hurt in battle during the Revolutionary War, she removed a musket ball herself with a penknife to avoid being discovered. During a hospitalization a year later, her identity was revealed. She eventually received an honorable discharge from the army.

Since the mid-nineteenth century, an undercurrent of feminism started to mature in the United States. American women were able to enjoy a public life, while the responsibility for children continued to be shared by both genders. The presence of women in private- and public-sector jobs has been increasing, although equal pay for equal work is still debated. There continues to be underrepresentation of women in Congress, despite the fact that more women seek public service.

In order to attract more females to political leadership, in 2011, the State Department partnered with several women colleges in the Women in Public Service Project to prepare future female leadership in our country and abroad. From 1789 to 2004, the United States had only elected white male presidents to lead our country. It took until 2008 for the first African American male to be elected and reelected in 2012. Still, the country favored a male candidate over a white female, who also ran for office.

Today, gender discrimination in the United States materializes in the workplace as unequal pay for equal work, and through the presence of a "glass ceiling," or inability for women to reach the top of the success ladder. These barriers are generally associated with family responsibilities, especially maternity and child rearing. Efforts, such as maternity or paternity leave and early childhood education programs, ameliorate the challenge for both genders, but do not eliminate the hurdles most women face.

Expectations about a woman's wardrobe, for instance, do not apply to men as well. Hillary Clinton's penchant for pantsuits was the center of ridicule by some during the 2016 presidential campaign, while her male opponents and counterparts escaped criticism regardless of what they chose to wear. If you watch women on TV, you will see a lot of short, tight skirts, in contrast to the conservative attire men generally sport.

These visuals underscore women's portrayal as sexualized objects, a fact that, in extreme cases, has brought about harassment and even rape. Not long ago, a powerful CEO of a major television network was forced to resign, and a popular conservative political pundit was fired, both under the specter of sexual harassment. Additionally, other powerful male celebrities have been condemned to long prison terms for sexual misconduct, including rape. With the aid of social media, these more severe forms of prejudice are more detectable and may no longer go unpunished.

A Fight for Gender Equality

It is an understatement to say that I have always been a strong advocate for gender equality. Physical attributes, strength, and height, rather than gender, should determine what individuals can or can't do. The gift of mind is not gender specific, so there should be no limits to women in this realm. I remember as a young girl tutoring a boyfriend in math. He was embarrassed, and I was playing it down, so as to keep from making him feel bad and definitely to keep from giving the impression that I was not feminine. It is amazing how effectively subliminal messages work!

Women have been making progress in the United States except in high political office. For the first time in 240 years, a woman, Hillary Clinton, was nominated for the presidency by a major political party. Vicious personal and professional attacks against her during her many years in public office were sufficient to ensure her defeat. She was running against a sexist, racist homophobe who exemplified a cartoonish version of an alpha male.

While Clinton campaigned by discussing specific policies that she would support as president, her male opponent seemed to be reading someone else's notes on the issues. Most of his time he dedicated his campaign speeches to degrading minorities, women, and anyone else who dared criticize him. Despite his many efforts to show he was unfit to become president, the Electoral College elected him forty-fifth president of the United States.

It is unfathomable that anyone would support the vitriol against women, whom this man derided by equating their worth to their sex appeal, calling them names such as "not a 10," a "fat pig," and worse. The 2016 election obviously did not resolve the place of women in our country, but it has generated incredible momentum for the future. Nationwide women's marches for equity, as well as the Me Too movement against the mistreatment of women, has brought millions of men, women, and children together in protest of unequal rights for women and minorities.

Guided by my mother's example, I maintain that education and a professional life in my new country allowed more choices and opportunities I would not have had otherwise. They have also freed me from the constraints of a role defined by others. I often think how different my days would have been if I had not left Cuba for a life in the United States, where independence and assertiveness are generally virtues and not targets of criticism.

By example, I try to instill my mother's message in my children and grandchildren. My greatest hope is that my granddaughters will soon be able to celebrate having been born women. If my dream is realized, it will definitely change the path of history, providing equal rights to those who have fallen victim to cultural genocide.

CHAPTER 6

REMEMBER WHEN

"The past beats inside me like a second heart" (John Banville, *The Sea*). Memories enhance our lives as witnesses of days lived. It is further rewarding to travel through memory lane and record some of these moments for the benefit of our children and grandchildren. I feel I owe it to them, as my recollections are part of their roots. Some memories humanize us; others simply make us smile. Their most important function is to finalize the portrayal of our life story.

As the third of four children, the only girl, I was destined for challenge. My older siblings played tricks on us, and my younger one encouraged me to get in trouble. Such was the day Rod persuaded me to climb a tree in front of the house, with the unfulfilled promise that he would join me. I was stuck up there, petrified and fuming. The predictable result was that I was caught and punished, while he reveled in his troublemaking skills.

Memories of loved ones we have lost bring their presence to the here and now. Reliving past remembrances does not have to be an unpleasant exercise. Many times, they offer glimpses of happy moments, making us smile all over again.

I have very early recollections of our big house on Avenida B and Calle 7, near the Jesuit school my father and brothers attended. Some of my earliest memories include a scene where my father is piercing my cousin's ears, and I am standing in my crib watching her screaming. What I thought at the time is not clear, but the image of the moment is just as vivid as if it had happened yesterday. Another memory of me looking down into the living room from a massive staircase dates back to 1944. I don't know if the view was as enormous as I recollect or if it was a factor of my being less than three feet tall and the world around me huge in comparison. At about the same time on my third birthday, I see myself standing on the porch with my beloved Tata waiting for my dad, who had promised to bring me a surprise present. To this day, the memory of my treasured red and blue wood scooter brings back a feeling of being special.

Me in the summer of 1944 at our home in B Avenue and 7th Street (B y 7)

Unpleasant thoughts of our past also play an important role, as sometimes they help uncover something significant about ourselves and others. In October 1944 a category 4 storm, known as the Cuba-Florida hurricane, hit western Cuba. In preparation, the family decided to stay at my aunt and uncle's home, equipped with a basement, which was an unusual feature in Cuban architecture.

The morning before the hurricane roared ashore, my father and I walked together the few blocks that separated the two houses. Though my dad was not a tall man, his stride was much longer than mine at age three.

So by the time we arrived at my aunt's, I was breathless. He was holding my hand, and I was also holding my much-loved satchel, filled with crayons and toys. I enjoyed playing school then, which is ironic considering how much I hated it a few years later when the game became a reality.

The family felt safe together in the midst of the threatening winds and rain. Candles, water, taped doors and windows—the adults seemed to know the drill, and we were ready for the storm. Flickering lights, darkness and the sound of an angry wind could have made the setting somber and fearful, but actually it was more like a party atmosphere. I also remember a lot of my cousins and other relatives joining the festive mood that did not match the impending danger. Cubans don't do well focusing on the bleak aspects of life, so a hurricane was no different, and as expected, a party ensued.

I just remember bits and pieces, but the story has been retold so many times, it feels real today. There was candlelight and music, provided by untrained voices and rhythm players, using furniture as instruments of sound. The result was not that bad, and it kept the revelers concentrating on enjoying the moment. Of course, there was dancing. Cubans are born with a dancing gene! At one point, my dad picked me up and let me look out the small basement window. We could see all kinds of debris flying past us, including a sofa and a palm tree, but I still felt safe in my father's arms.

The hurricane was devastating to the western part of the island. My family survived, but our home was damaged irreparably. Doors flew off their hinges and, along with them, clothing, furnishings, and whatever other items were in the path of the wind and rain. Mother's closet was emptied, and in the midst of what could have been a tragedy, there was humor. We think one of my mother's girdles was found hanging from an electric pole across from the neighborhood convenient store. The object became the talk of the town, but thankfully its owner remained anonymous—until now.

Destiny, Karma, and "que sera, será" are compelling phenomena. My future husband was born and raised across the street from the house where I was born. Our parents knew each other, since my father was their physician. Our future was sealed, as both families supported the idea of a marriage. He was five years older than I was, and our paths would not cross until I was in my late teens. After the hurricane, we moved away from that address to the Vedado neighborhood (Calle 17 entre 14 y 16), also in Havana, where my father had his medical practice in the first floor and our living quarters upstairs.

Rod dressed as a Canadian Mounted Police in our Vedado home, 1945

There are so many fond memories of these years, including my father's nurse who did most of my homework during my elementary school years.

By then, my youngest brother Rod, who was twenty months younger than I, was my best buddy. We converted a turkey crate, into an office equipped with my aluminum toy typewriter and a play phone. We felt we were ready for business.

It was amusing to play with Rod and pretend we were Hopalong Cassidy, his favorite cowboy, and Dale Evans, mine. We spent an inordinate amount of time fighting imaginary wars and riding imaginary horses. The two of us would alternate our make-believe worlds from protectors of the law to surgeons or actors.

Rod and I in 1947

Our poor mother had to deal with my extensive and expensive doll collection covered in Merthiolate and bandages, evidence of our dexterity as "surgeons." As actors, we would prepare a puppet show with scripts of our own and invite our friends. It did not work as a moneymaking venture, but once we stopped charging five cents, it became more popular. There were many amusing stories surrounding my little brother, who no doubt was a genius.

While we lived in Vedado, our parents enrolled us in preprimary and kindergarten at a Catholic school nearby. It was run by Spanish nuns, who believed that harsh discipline would make us better kids. This belief did not go over well with us, and our tears and protestations convinced our parents that they should find a school that would be a better fit. They also feared having a couple of very early dropouts on their hands. Mother understood well that learning might not take place without enjoyment of the process, so new schools were found.

Since Catholic schooling was important to my parents, I was enrolled in the same American Dominican Academy my mother had attended as a child. For us, schools were a family affair, since the various generations received their education from the same institution. Although this school had less rigorous discipline, I still disliked it. But I managed to endure all my elementary grades. Oh, how much I hated school then! I was bored with the pace and the assignments and feared the discipline. It was hard to stay in my seat and concentrate, so I traveled around the room and chatted with my friends, to the exasperation of the nuns.

Patience has never been my middle name, and most of the time, I was either reprimanded or forced to stand up facing the wall. At the end of second grade, I did not get the customary medals or certificates my classmates received, but I was still promoted to the next grade. The humiliating experience seemed to help in my turn around.

In my Dominican Academy uniform, but not looking very happy

In retrospect, I would probably have been diagnosed with attention deficit and hyperactive disorder, since staying on task and paying attention were difficult for me. I don't know how much my parents were informed of my objectionable behavior at school, but I do not remember it being an issue at home. At the time, it was written off as boredom.

Although discipline methods were more lenient than those experienced early on as a kindergartener, I felt disconnected. I thought of myself as a small island surrounded by strangers who were not even aware of my presence. My best friend was Toty Herrera, oldest child of my parents' good friends Benito and Kety. She was not only taller and prettier, but she was also a much better student. I was always on the losing end of inevitable comparisons. Despite that, Toty and I were joined at the hip. On some occasions, our parents would dress us alike, as if we were twins. Many times, I would stay with the Herreras after school, and Aunt Muma would help us with our school projects. I thoroughly enjoyed our times together.

My life took a positive turn in the third grade, when as part of a talent show, I dubbed famous 1920's Broadway star Al Jolson. My rendition of "Mammy" earned me a standing ovation, with the nuns doubled up in laughter. As an encore, I chose "California Here I Come," resulting in an increase in popularity and instant fame among my peers. After the experience, my behavior improved, allowing me to complete my elementary grades without any further tribulation.

The taste of public adoration made me interested in acting. A child actor rode in the same school bus I did, and I was starstruck. An opportunity came to be a guest on a children's puppet show, *The Camejo Brothers*, and my Aunt Niní handmade a puppet for me, the Spanish *señorita*, which I dearly loved. My first appearance on TV went well, and it was followed by an offer of a bit part in a Cuban movie about José Martí, the patriot and literary figure. My father's horror at having his daughter become an actress put an end to my silver screen dreams. Not much was lost, as acting was not really my forte!

I encountered the meaning of death when my eight-year-old friend Peggy passed away, a victim of leukemia. She was a very smart, very sweet little girl with an incredibly positive attitude in facing her lot. We loved chatting, going for long walks around the neighborhood, and simply enjoying each other's company. Gentle-natured Peggy never complained and never showed fear; instead, she always had a ready smile.

The realization that she was gone was a shocker. As we passed Peggy's home while returning from a trip, I was shaken to see a hearse parked in front. I knew that very instant my little friend was gone, and they were taking her away. Her death left a void in my life. How could death happen to a kid? I became frightened that I would die the same way, and it took a long time for me to accept death without fear.

Peggy's passing was the beginning of my loss of innocence. Having never had a serious conversation with my significant adults regarding the birds and the bees, life's secrets came as a shock when a young maid took it upon herself to describe in graphic detail the particulars of intercourse. Rather than feeling thrilled, I felt repulsed with the conversation. It took me a while to look at boys without feeling shame. The young maid left the family before I was able to notify my parents, so they never suspected that Santa Claus, the Tooth Fairy, and the Stork were no longer part of my belief system.

My first bike brought me joy and a lesson learned. Mother was of the belief that children needed to dream. She felt that yearning was healthy, as it made us appreciate what we wished for, once attained. At age seven, I wanted a bicycle desperately after my best friend got hers for her birthday. Mother figured that Christmas would be a better time, as waiting would make me dream a bit longer, plan, get excited, and finally more appreciative of the gift. I don't know how many times I woke up from a dream in which I had been riding my bike. Christmas finally arrived, and to this moment, I still see my red and black bike under the tree. I also remember the amazing feeling of a dream come true.

As a child, I had two responsibilities—having fun and going to school. In my bubble, there was no other reality, despite the fact that history was happening all around us. On March 10, 1952, a coup d'état brought General Fulgencio Batista to power for the second time. My little brother and I did not understand the ramifications of this political change. We were innocently enjoying days off school, just like we often did when hurricanes came to shore. Little did we know that, less than seven years later, a new dictator, Fidel Castro, would force us to abandon our homeland.

As I was growing up, pets were always a part of the family—a parrot, a monkey, several turtles, two dogs, a horse, and twenty-seven cats! Rita, the parrot, did not stay long with us, as she would not allow a dinner conversation without her loud mocking of everyone. The neighbor across the street, a widower, adopted Rita and was able to give her the pampered existence she deserved. The cats were feral and lived outside but surprisingly enjoyed playing and being petted.

My oldest brother was papa to the dogs. Of the two, Lady was the queen. She descended from champion pointer lines but behaved like a sweet mutt. Smart and affectionate, Lady had a loving home, and she reveled in it. Prince, the boxer, was another story. He was not as well behaved as Lady; we had to make sure our plates were off the table, or he would claim them as his own. We loved him though. Inside the tough looks lived a gentle, albeit mischievous soul.

The monkey, which was named Ulysses, had a fascinating background. He came from dictator Anastasio Somoza's family in Nicaragua via a cousin who had attended finishing school in New York with one of his girls. When my cousin returned to Cuba with a monkey, she met with her mom's firm resistance to adopt him. We begged ours to let us keep Ulysses, and to our surprise, she acquiesced. I had illusions of having him dressed up in a suit, joining our family dinner. To my chagrin, this never took place.

Ulysses happened to be a sneaky escape artist, who preferred to run down the street with one of us in pursuit. Soon, we realized that Ulysses belonged in the wild. A good friend of the family wanted to have the monkey on his ten-acre farm, so we all agreed this was a better life for our pet. Ironically, we later found out he was a she. Hence, she was renamed Christina, in honor of the first well-known transgender, Dr. Christina Jorgensen.

When my brother Carlos left Cuba in 1959, he gave me Princess, a beautiful Tennessee walker. She was an award-winning mare with a gait as royal as her name. My Saturdays were dedicated to wonderful backcountry rides with her trainer and my dad riding a small stallion he had bought for these occasions. This experience is ingrained in me as a spiritual connection with my horse, the woods, and with the two people who shared these magical moments.

There were several near misses during my childhood. Having three energetic brothers, I found playing baseball with their male friends a forbidden enjoyment, as genders would not usually meet in play. On a day that we had staged a game in front of our home, my father appeared, and appeared shocked! His little girl at bat with a field full of boys was a scandal in his mind. What would the neighbors think of the family allowing their most precious jewel to play with boys? What saved my day was a black eye suffered when I missed a fly ball.

Although a lot of pampering followed, that was definitely the end of my short-lived baseball career. I gave losing an eye another chance in a visit to Central Limones, the sugar mill administered by Toty's dad. During those stays, we would enjoy the freedom of nature and the fun of horseback riding—that is, until my horse veered into a lemon tree. My right eye missed the twin thorns that managed to scrape my face and leave me with another black eye.

My parents and I were relieved, although my First Holy Communion was to take place two weeks later, and the discoloration was still prominent. My lovely white organza dress, flowered tiara, white gloves, and old family rosary were not enough distractions to hide the bruises.

Memories of Easter celebrations during those years were many. Starting about age five, I participated in religious pilgrimages dressed as an angel. My first experience was not quite pleasant, when I became frightened by another youngster dressed as Saint Michael, the archangel. His shiny armor and cardboard sword seemed ominous at the time. Holding the hand of a terrified little angel, Tata marched for quite a few blocks in the scorching Havana sun, so I could participate in the procession.

The expression tells the story. The "angel" in 1945

It was customary at the Dominican school to encourage sacrifice during Advent and indicate achievement by placing a straw in baby Jesus's manger. I had heard that, in Mexico, the faithful would walk into church on their knees as a sign of devotion. It seemed like a good idea at the time to suggest to a few of my friends to go to the chapel and do just that.

I was not counting on how hysterical it was to see bobbing heads in a row making the rounds. We were all having fits of laughter, having to take breaks to regain our composure. Little did we know, Sister Mary Daniels was observing the show, arms crossed and trying to contain her reactions to the sidesplitting sight. Needless to say, no straws were placed for our effort, but Sister MD did not have the heart to punish us.

Good Fridays were spent attending an austere service and abstaining from eating any kind of meat. The tone was somber, a reminder of Jesus's crucifixion. Particularly daunting for a youngster, the atmosphere caused our nerves to get the best of us. Nothing was more painful than to try to maintain equanimity, when our body really wanted to guffaw. Trying to think of something sad and pinching ourselves were not enough in our attempts to stop our hysterics. Invariably, we ended up being taken outside.

As I said before, love came early in my life. At twelve years old, I fell head over heels in love with Pablito, the grandson of my father's patient and good friend, Eulogio González. Fun-filled, innocent times followed, until growing apart ended the romance but not the wholesome memories.

I had thought my childhood had been uneventful. But in retrospect, living through hurricanes, heartbreaks, revolution, and a zest for adventure make me realize that being able to continue my journey in one piece was nothing short of a miracle.

High School Memories and My Teens

Early in my teenage years, I was a ship without a compass, not knowing how I related to the rest of the universe or even what I meant to others. I cannot say I was a happy camper, since I was always being compared to my best friend. We looked very different, and I always felt I was at a disadvantage. Comparisons in children generally leave scars. By Cuban standards, I should have been the winner of this unnecessary contest, but Mother's obsession with weight and height made me feel otherwise. Given that Mother was barely five feet and my dad just a few inches taller, her expectations about me had no basis in reality.

I spent my early teens in a well-known endocrinologist's office, Dr. Julio Schutte, losing weight and even attempting a new treatment that would help prepubescent youngsters in gaining height. The treatments stopped when I developed headaches, and my father grew concerned about the possibility of a brain tumor. I acquired a few inches but, most of all, an aversion to weight gain. I became a mental anorexic, although, fortunately, my eating habits remained healthy. It has taken me a lifetime to rid myself of the negative feelings when carrying extra pounds.

Now, I invoke the words of my psychiatrist friend, Dr. Tony Rubio, regarding his acceptance of his own battle of the bulge: "I have declared myself fat, so I enjoy whatever I eat or drink without guilt."

A product of a culture that protects girls' virginity 24/7, I was a naive creature during my teens. Young women who lost their virginity before the wedding night were deemed damaged goods and were not considered good candidates for matrimony. I enjoyed many boyfriends, and holding hands or a chaste kiss met the requirements. My female friends and I remained children to a certain extent, and our innocence was sheltered at all cost. After all, the dignity of a family name relied on the virtues of the younger females.

My parents loved each other but also enjoyed occasional arguments. In later years, I realized that my mother had inherited the gene of being contrary. Mother and her siblings enjoyed a good squabble, even if the topic was inane. Father, on the other hand, took pleasure in setting up the subject matter and retiring to enjoy the debate that ensued, just like a chess game.

Once at the breakfast table with ultraconservative Fernando and I, Father started a discussion about religion. And as expected, my brother and I took opposing sides of the issues. As the argument became more vivid, my father whispered in my ear, "Don't argue about religion with your brother. That is all he has." I realized my father had declared me the victor in this odd chess game.

As it is often common among youngsters, I lived with the fear that my parents would divorce. Fortunately, my anxiety was unwarranted. They remained husband and wife until my mother's death in 1976, having celebrated their golden wedding anniversary just a few months before. I learned that the meaning of a relationship can only be measured by those involved and that individuals fulfill needs in each other that no outsider can understand or explain.

Mother and Father celebrating their golden wedding
anniversary in Houston, Summer 1974

During those years, I was terribly afraid of dying. This could have been because, as a family, we lived so close to the life-and-death experiences my father faced on a daily basis. It could have also been due to the untimely loss of my friend Peggy, a child whose life promise was denied. Whatever the reason, I became a hypochondriac—afraid every little ache was a sign of something ominous. Fortunately, my patient father was on hand to appease me, but I must have driven him crazy with my concerns about imaginary ailments. As it happens to many teens, emotional issues can be of a temporary nature, and luckily, I was able to outgrow my phobias.

It helped that, during my high school years, I developed an outgoing personality. I discovered the power of humor and claimed my parents' funny bone. My many friends seemed to like me, and I never hurt for company or adventure. I went from, "Is this all there is?" to having lots of innocent fun with my ever-growing number of friends.

Even a funeral could become a source of unexpected giggles. When our friend Olga's grandfather passed away, a group of us decided to visit the funeral home together. Cold, but elegantly appointed, Caballero Funeral Home was the choice of many Havana families who had suffered the loss of a loved one. As Elvira, Carmina, Zaira, and I entered the elevator, we felt clammy, nervous with anticipation. Suddenly, unstoppable giggles took over. When the doors opened to the chapel, the fragrance of a sea of flowers and a tableau in black helped us regain self-control.

We located Olga, who seemed eager to talk to us. "My grandfather did not die," she blurted out.

In split seconds, I thought her grandfather had awakened and left the mourners to pay respect to an empty casket.

Almost concurrently, Olga added, "He committed suicide."

"What a relief," were the words that flew out of my mouth.

Fortunately, Olga had been pulled aside by her mother, so she never heard the exchange. The giggles returned, and the four of us had to make an abrupt exit. The beauty of being a teen is that we are oblivious to any responsibility beyond having a good time, even in the most outlandish of circumstances.

The teen years have also been known as challenging times, as individuals are making a transition from childhood to pre-adulthood. The world does not conform to the self-centered worldview of most teenagers. For the most part, we see ourselves as the center of the universe, with others there to enhance our lives. As the teens progress, our relationship to others transform into interactions, as if for the first time we realize we are not independent beings. I started wanting to impress others and seeking my friends' approval to win their friendship. I worked hard at it and succeeded in making and keeping my friends.

We lived near Tropicana Nightclub during part of my teens. I remember on Valentine's Day hearing Nat King Cole serenading his audience. The music was delightfully transmitted on clear nights to the entire neighborhood. Our next-door neighbors, the López family enjoyed weekend dancing parties with at least three generations in attendance.

My younger brother Rod and I were the stars of the show, as we had mastered fifties classics, such as Elvis's "Hound Dog," and Bill Haley & His Comets' "Rock Around the Clock."

So dancing and humor were my talents and "fun-loving Andreíta" was born, which also happened to be the caption used in the 1958 yearbook with my graduation picture. Although I did not think so then, I was cute, funny, and a great dancer. So my phone did not stop ringing. There was a time when mother got quite confused taking a message for me, as I was dating three Miguels and two Manuels at the same time! Dating in Cuba simply meant going to a movie, a dinner or both, always in the company of an adult chaperone.

I only became a serious student when I attended another American school. Ruston Academy, a high-school experience filled with warm-hearted memories of good friends and great times. Ruston, as a preparatory school with high academic standards, was just what I needed to make me a student. How I was able to make the transition from not ever cracking a book during my elementary grades to becoming a dedicated student is inexplicable.

It is also ironic that as a person who had once hated school, I would spend the rest of my life as a student completing three degrees and later as a teacher. In essence, I never left school!

At Ruston, it was not cool to be an indifferent student. Good grades and discipline were important requisites to endure the rigor of the new educational environment. I also learned to deal with my undiagnosed attention deficit disorder, because my survival depended on it. Choosing Ruston told me Mother had seen the future and had wanted me to be prepared. I was not only improving English communication skills but also learning about accepted behaviors and nuances of the American culture.

While attending Ruston, I made some great friends, Zaira, Elvira, and Olga. We became an inseparable quartet that intermixed study and fun, both intensely. Having been five before Teresita got married and left school, we had named our exclusive group "Punjab," meaning "land of the five rivers" in India. We kept the name and created a modified Spanish version of "pig Latin" to communicate among ourselves. There was also a group of boys, Andrés, Alejandro, Ramiro, Willy, and Jack, who became our dates, when parties called. Those were, by far, the happiest years of my life in Cuba, although after graduation in 1958, the Castro Revolution was well underway.

The Punjab on Graduation night, June 1958
From left to right: Zaira, Elvira, me and Olga

There were many other Rustonians I remember fondly. One was Puchy Calvo, who became a very close friend during our first years in exile. She had it all—classy; elegant; petite; absolutely beautiful; and, above all, really funny. We were in the same public speaking class in high school, from which I have very fond memories, particularly of a show-and-tell activity that she forgot to prepare. On her way out the door that morning, Puchy thought of the assignment, and she just grabbed the first interesting gadget she saw on their bar. It was the figure of a clown that could perform all kinds of functions, such as opening bottles and cans while playing an upbeat circus melody.

Our class was early that morning, and Puchy was the first presenter. She was sounding confident, and we were all amused with her explanations, until she pressed a button she had not seen before. To her bafflement, the corkscrew popped up, suggestive of a certain male anatomical feature. She tried to press it down to no avail, and by now she had lost the class, including the instructor, to total hysterics.

She left the podium as quickly as she could, and spent the rest of the day carrying the clown around, covered with her sweater because it would not fit in her locker. She paid the price for a risky improvisation, but left an indelible memory.

We experienced many moments of shared innocent mischief—delightful memories that bring a smile when recounted. We were the terror of substitute teachers when passing around a small box that meowed if turned and enjoyed testing our PE teacher's sanity as we marched in the opposite direction from what she had indicated. Our class favorite, however, was getting Olga's desk on top of an armoire, while she pretended nothing was amiss. Unfortunately, that mischief did not turn out as planned, when our instructor Dr. Beatriz Varela completely ignored the incident. After a short while, we started feeling silly, especially Olga. These were moments that got us into a bit of trouble with our principal and teachers—trouble that was worth the memories it created.

Ruston's Girl Basketball Team, 1957
(I am third from left in front row, next to Elvira. Straight behind us, Zaira and Olga)

During my third year of Bachillerato (our version of high school, which requires five years of study), Mother thought that it would be a great educational experience to send me abroad for a year. I lived in Washington, DC, with my Aunt Niní and my godmother while attending eighth grade at Sacred Heart parochial school.

I was a bit older than my classmates, but I was getting immersed in the language and the culture of the United States, including square dancing and basketball. I proved to be a fierce guard, which gained me the nickname "Long Sam," an attractive dark-haired comic strip heroine popular at the time.

When I returned to Cuba at the end of the school year, my Ruston classmates had moved on to the next grade, so my parents hired a tutor during the summer to prepare me to take exams for each course. After completing additional entrance exams, I was successful in skipping the year I had missed. Our last two years at Ruston were the most memorable. They did not include drugs, alcohol, or any serious mischief, just the pure enjoyment of youth among friends.

We mostly dated our classmates and had great times together. One afternoon, we were in Jack's brand-new blue convertible, sailing through the streets of Havana. We heard a siren, and next thing, we were being stopped by a police officer. After the officer had recognized Jack's address as that of his five-star general dad, Jack received an apology rather than a fine. That was my first experience with governmental privilege and corruption. Not long after, Batista and his men had resigned and left the country. We never saw or heard from Jack again after that.

All of us, with the exception of Zaira, left Cuba eventually. We had been told her parents were divorced, so that explained to us why we had never met her dad. The truth was he had been a pro-Castro revolutionary in hiding, who eventually surfaced very much alive and still married to her mom. Zaira joined the Communist militia after we left, and I never saw or heard from her again, until I went to the University of Guadalajara in 1995 as an exchange faculty.

I was staying where five Cuban professors resided, while teaching at the same place. I was a bit apprehensive to meet them, as I had never personally encountered any Communist Cubans. To my surprise, they were delighted to meet a fellow Cuban, and politics never entered our conversations. One of them, Mirta, was a philosopher, so I asked her if, perchance, she knew Zaira, who had shown an interest in majoring in philosophy. Her answer stunned me. "Are you kidding me? She was the most important philosopher of the revolution."

Sadly, my friend had died in a tragic accident in 1986, but Mirta gifted me with one of the many books Zaira had written. My missing friend Zaira Rodríguez Ugidos had become a leading philosopher of Marxism and professor of philosophy at the University of Havana, until her untimely death. It did not totally surprise me that her work had become emblematic of Marxism-Leninism.

I remember that, during our junior year, Zaira attended La Sorbonne in Paris, and she came back transformed. For a reason I can't recollect, we had gone to church together after her return, and she had refused to kneel throughout the lengthy service. When asked, she simply responded, "I don't believe in God." The conversation ended there.

Elvira (Bibi) moved to Panama, married a Panamanian, and had three children. She became a psychologist, although her first love, while at school, was chemistry.

Divorced with children and grandchildren, Olga (Olguita) moved to upstate New York after receiving a PhD from Harvard. While I was Dean of Academic Affairs at Miami Dade College, I invited her to present her memoir *Scatter My Ashes Over Havana* to students and faculty. In attendance were two of our high school teachers and several of our classmates. It was a wonderful reconnection, and of course, we spent all of our time reminiscing about our days at Ruston.

Regarding the boys, Alejandro and Willy still live in Miami with their families after retirement, but sadly we have lost Andrés and Evelio. We never found out about Jack's fate. I called him on December 31, 1958, to wish him a happy New Year. He and his family left secretly for exile the next day, along with other military leaders in the Batista army.

Ruston provided us with the tools to successfully navigate life in the United States. No matter the distance between us or the destiny we have each faced, we will always be Rustonians.

CHAPTER 7

IN SEARCH OF FREEDOM

It was about 7:30 p.m. on a Friday evening in Havana, February 1959. Family, friends, and neighbors were congregated on our spacious porch. Several generations were enjoying the innocent banter and colorful storytelling. We had heard some of the stories many times, but with each retelling they seemed to get better. At about 9:30, he showed up—again.

He was a *miliciano* with his best friend a *metralleta* (machine gun), arriving to remind us that we were past the curfew. "Se acabó. Son más de las nueve." (It's over. It's past nine.) The words he used sounded ominous: "It's over."

Indeed, those innocent times with family and friends were a thing of the past. Cubans had lost control of their lives, and the new government owned our destiny. Choices had been replaced with laws that dictated our every word, our every action.

That was my life in Cuba after 1959, and living it compromised my very being.

The Time Has Come

Few people born and raised in the United States take the time to be thankful for their freedoms to be true to self or to be able think and act without fear of persecution. For some of us, who escaped repressive governments, freedom is a gift beyond description. The oppression of the Castro Cuba took away our tranquility. We lived in fear. Imprisonment, death penalties liberally handed out, and fearmongering kept most of us in line. Besides home searches and curfews, it was not uncommon for the officials to plant evidence or simply threaten us for acting in ways that displeased them.

Early on, laws were passed restricting travel from Cuba. Leaving the country meant that all the possessions left behind belonged to the government. An inventory detailing one's property was required, and after its official submission, nothing could be moved from the house under penalty of imprisonment.

Once the "list" was checked by the authorities, one might be free to leave the country. Mother was fearless enough to challenge the law and managed to replace her inventory with similar items of lesser value. She swapped a functioning color TV with a defective set, replaced towels and sheets with raggedy ones, and left behind furniture that was quite worn. She survived defying the law, unscathed.

Many people would not arrive home from work or play. They were detained or jailed for a few days due to fitting the profile of a *gusano* (worm), a name given to those of us who disagreed with the new order. On his way home after work, my cousin, Gustavo de los Reyes was detained and sent to jail. His family, not having heard from him, dreaded the worst.

The authorities had planted a phone number in his pocket that belonged to a "person of interest," someone my cousin had never met. Fortunately, just as he was detained without any explanation, he was released after a few days in captivity. Soon after, Gustavo, his wife, and their four children left Cuba.

An unsettling experience happened one day at the University of Havana. A couple of friends and I were harmlessly walking in the first floor of our school, when a gigantic Cuban flag fell from the third floor, engulfing us in a red, blue, and white mountain of fabric. We were disoriented and horrified by the dark and heavy attacker but were successful in freeing ourselves with some effort. We were received on the other side by three armed *milicianos* pointing their weapons at us, demanding an explanation. We had no idea what had happened or how, and luckily, it became clear to them that we were not the guilty party that had caused the mayhem. Our hearts were pounding, and our nerves brought forth the inconvenient giggles. Fortunately, the officers were too busy dealing with the monstrous flag to pay attention to three hysterical students.

There were so many close calls. It was not uncommon to unexpectedly run into shootouts, in the streets, in a bus, almost anywhere. We became experts in taking cover. Our everyday lives involved the risk of trying to lead a normal life. Not being safe, even at home, became part of our daily undertakings.

It was also annoying that, when making a phone call, we had to suffer a recording—"*Patria o muerte; venceremos*" (Country or death; we shall conquer)—before we could dial out. It was a cruel reminder that freedom of speech was no longer a right. We had to become inventive in saying what we wanted to, by using creative metaphors to confuse the anonymous listener. The United States became *la finca de Germán* (Herman's farm). Uncle Herman lived in Miami, so visiting *la finca de Germán* meant to us leaving for the United States. When you are forced to speak in metaphors to protect your right to free speech, life becomes a constant struggle.

An unexpected knock on the door would translate into another visit from the militia. On one occasion, the *milicianos* went directly to our garage and, without apology, confiscated my Uncle Jorge's car. How they knew that it was there remains an unsettling mystery. Someone had obviously reported the car to the authorities, someone close to us. Was it a friend? A family member? A neighbor? Who had been brainwashed? We never found out. The new regime taught citizens that their first loyalty was not to family, but to government. We lived doubting everyone, and fearing we would be in line for reprisal. It was hard to feel safe, when we never knew if our next move was on solid ground, or the entryway to an abyss.

Image of Che Guevara on a Cuban Coin

Once Fidel Castro was pronounced a victor, the mass exodus and televised trials of public officials were added to our bleak reality. His imposing figure, added to his beyond belief gift of gab, made him an instant hero to some. Havana, like the rest of the island, was inundated with bearded, long-haired officers (the *barbudos*), who had fought side by side with Castro.

Those who felt they had nothing to hide turned themselves in, only to find out that they had been declared "enemies of the state." One of those was mild-mannered Colonel Mario Menéndez (Mayito), my brother Carlos' brother-in-law. Mayito had been assistant to President Batista, but had never played a significant role in governmental decisions. I attended his trial, and was able to witness the concept of justice of the new order. Mayito, whose girlfriend was expecting a child, and four other men, received a life sentence without any evidence of wrongdoing.

Lt. Colonel Mario Menéndez Domingo, in light uniform behind
President Batista and the First Lady, circa 1958

My brother Carlos; his wife, Marta; and their four-year old son went into hiding. Marta was the niece of Batista's prime minister, who had also served as interim president, while Batista ran for office. Marta's uncle had already left Cuba; her oldest brother was in prison; and the rest of her family was also in hiding, hoping for a safe escape.

My poor mother was devastated. At first there was no news about Carlos' whereabouts. But as soon as we knew, I became the family's messenger. I felt like a spy, walking down a street with a crumpled message in my hand that was to be exchanged with one from a stranger walking in the opposite direction. I knew him only as "the skinny guy with a red cap." Had I been caught, I would have probably become a statistic.

We considered ourselves lucky that my brother and his family were able to leave the country without any added complications. My mother was sad but relieved, and now she only had a husband and three other children to consider. Her greatest worry was my brother Fernando, who could not control himself when the frequent militia searches of our home took place. One of the officers turned to Mother, cautioning her about Fernando's protests, "Tell your son to watch his mouth, if he wants to avoid consequences."

Her concerns became overwhelming, and at that moment, she decided she would stay in Cuba until all her chickens had safely flown the coop. The image of *milicianos*, weapons drawn, "searching" our home is etched in my mind. I cringe every time I think about it.

No day would pass without receiving bad news about someone. Televised trials, including the administration of death penalties, served as warnings for what could happen if we were not allies. The *paredón* (wall where prisoners were shot to death) was the usual punishment for those deemed traitors.

Fear and distrust marked our days on the island. Curfews were ordered, so 8:00 a.m. to 9:00 p.m. became our daily schedule. To live without freedoms is to be half-dead. My day was church, school, and boyfriend. Parties stopped, and so did any kind of celebration. I also stopped trusting my friends, who were leaving the country one by one.

My neighbor Silvia was engaged to a *barbudo*, so I was afraid of what to share with her. Another friend, Margarita, also a classmate, would drive us to school. I did not know then that she and her husband Alberto were involved in counterrevolutionary activities, so the trip to the university was a risk we did not know we were taking. Many years later and already in exile, she confessed that, during one of my visits to their home, a man sought by Castro was hiding in one of their bedrooms—another close call! In retrospect, we were luckier than a cat with nine lives to be able to escape our country in one piece. We soon realized that the only way to survive was to leave.

Easier said than done! Restrictions were placed when leaving the country, which only became more stringent as time passed. To leave was to give up what was familiar for a world unknown. At the time we left, the government officials required a credible reason, and a round-trip ticket as evidence of a planned return. We used our honeymoon as an excuse and proceeded to plan the departure. Before then, there had to be a wedding.

Plans to marry in summer 1960 were made in the midst of a revolution that would forever change our destiny. Preparations started, and it all seemed quite normal for the wedding of the only girl in the family. The most expensive item would be the dress, which seemed to be the greatest waste.

As luck would have it, my sister-in-law had worn an incredible dress and tiara designed by Bernabeu, a well-known couturier of the rich and famous. She was eager to let me wear it, but there was only one problem. She was a size 4, and I was a 10! At first, I thought only a miracle could make this happen, but a wonderful family member, Siria Cardoso de Pasalodos, a talented seamstress, came to my rescue.

Other arrangements were less challenging, except securing the documents required for our departure. Visas were not so easy to obtain. But Mother, the expert in obtaining the unobtainable, spoke to a well-connected priest, who helped us procure the paperwork. I remember the cloak-and-dagger atmosphere surrounding the event. We went to a dark old church in Old Havana to meet with some unknown man in the sacristy of the church. Although I did not see it, I assume money exchanged hands, and our visas were granted at high-speed.

August 5, 1960, arrived, and, on that day, I was to become a married woman. As I was getting ready for the event, our friend Siria became the person in charge of dressing me. After all, she deserved the honor, since she was able to make the size four dress large enough for the new bride. I remember her soothing voice, while we shared a cup of *tilo* (linden tea).

I was excited but not nervous, although there had not been a sighting of the groom at the church, and it was getting late. He did make his entrance, better late than never, so my father and I got ready for our much-anticipated arrival.

Arriving at church with my father

We had chosen the Church of Corpus Christi, a beautiful example of gothic architecture, but not too big as to make the bride and the groom disappear in comparison. My dad looked so handsome and proud his only girl was marrying a nice boy from a well-known family. I am not sure anyone thought how lucky the groom actually was!

As we walked down the aisle, I remember seeing my friends standing on the sides with beautiful smiles that were hiding the reality of the moment. This was the last time we were to see each other.

Making our entrance at the Corpus Christi Church, August 5, 1960

In the distance, the smiling groom and the two mothers dressed to the hilt awaited our arrival. Beautiful white roses, whose fragrance I can still smell, and music, including Titahita's beautiful rendition of Gounod's *Ave Maria*, welcomed us after we made our entrance. Her voice was still magnificent, and her singing made my heart sad and happy at the same time.

Two weeks after the wedding ceremony and after a short honeymoon, we found ourselves getting ready for our departure. Although it was a sad moment for us, we felt at the time it was a temporary solution. Little did we know.

The Infamous Airport

The José Martí International Airport had a special significance for exiled Cubans. It marked an event in our journey to freedom that was an end and a beginning. It was a moment that held our future captive as the die was cast. Once at the airport, we feared retaliation and wondered if we were going to be allowed to board or ordered to stay. There were many stories of harassment and worse. Many were held in Cuba against their wishes for only one reason—to harass those seeking exile, considered by the authorities as *merengues* (softies).

José Martí International Airport

It is an understatement to say that leaving the country was not easy. When my husband of two weeks and I left Cuba in 1960, officials would select two people among the passengers and conduct a thorough, invasive, and undignified search. The fear that you would be chosen was enough discouragement to taking anything of value out of the country. Mementos had to stay behind, because they would confiscate even your family photos. We were lucky that we were not chosen, but the two unfortunate passengers looked unnerved.

Some airport experiences turned comedic, but most of them were stories of humiliation and harassment. My friend María's parents, Dr. Rafael and Lilian Santamaría, were bringing their five-month old daughter Annie, since their other six children had been sent earlier to the United States in the Peter Pan Operation. The Santamarías could board on the condition that they leave Annie behind. At the last minute, they were requiring a passport for the infant, a requirement that had been added on the spot. That was out of the question, but there was little money could not fix, so they finally were allowed to leave with Annie.

However, Mrs. Santamaría was wearing a valuable pearl necklace that had been her grandmother's. The heirloom attracted the eye of the immigration officer. "How about what you are wearing?" he asked without preamble.

Mrs. Santamaría, with the courage you gain in moments like this, convincingly responded, "Oh, you can have it! It's a cheap old thing."

The man lost his interest and let her board the plane with her priceless treasures.

There were countless other stories similar to the Santamarías. After the Bay of Pigs, my colleague and friend Margarita Oteiza went to Cuba to claim her husband's remains. He was one of the heroes of the invasion, when his group of four men had escaped their sinking ship while at battle with the Castro forces. Although Alberto was a champion swimmer, energy failed him before he could reach shore. Days later, a fisherman discovered his body and took him to the authorities for proper burial.

My friend Margarita was able to locate the fisherman and receive a witness account of Alberto González Recio's tragic end. The fisherman also gave her his watch and wedding ring. At the airport en route to the United States, she was wearing both. They were special remembrances she had from him, but they attracted the attention of the immigration officer. "You can go," he said, "but the watch and the ring stay here."

Margarita, elegant, classy, and towering over the official, responded without a speck of fear, "You will have to kill me to get them. They belonged to my late husband, and that is all that remains of him."

There must have been some decency left in the man, as he allowed her on the plane with her husband's personal effects.

What motivated Cubans to seek refuge elsewhere was a thirst for freedom, a basic need to create our own future. We were inspired by the words of Kahlil Gibran, "Life without liberty is like a body without spirit" (*The Vision: Reflections in the Way of the Soul*).

CHAPTER 8

ON THE BRINK OF ADULTHOOD: MY TWENTIES, A DECADE OF "FIRSTS"

The decade of my twenties was memorable—marriage, exile, motherhood, and so much more. A "fall from innocence" would be an understatement, as adulthood came calling with a loud bang. My teens were disrupted by my first marriage, by the Castro Revolution, and by our eventual exile. What a way to wake up from what we thought was an endless dream. A naive teenager, who had lived a well-protected life in her native land, had to suddenly face new responsibilities with very few survival tools at her disposal.

The last two years of my teens were a flurry of activities. I graduated from Ruston in June 1958 and was accepted to the School of Architecture at the Catholic University of Villanova in Havana. I was thrilled to follow in the path of several family architects, Rodrigo Saavedra, Senior and Junior; my godfather Manolo de los Reyes; and cousin José Manuel García-Lavín (Joche).

My entrance exam consisted of tests measuring knowledge of physics and mathematics, as well as artistic skills. The first part was not much of a challenge, as Ruston Academy had prepared me well. Drawing gave me pause. I realized how outperformed I was by my future classmates. Their versions were complex and artistic; mine was a flowerpot! I went home a bit worried that perhaps I would not make it, but news was good, and I managed to be accepted.

Unfortunately, by spring 1959, Castro's revolution had taken over the government, and the Catholic University was closed. My dream of ever becoming an architect was lost forever.

My short-lived days as a budding architect were fun, with the exception of a course in architectural drawing. I spent many sleepless nights seated at my drawing table fighting with my T-ruler and compass to complete my assignments. The task required attention to detail and patience, two traits I lacked. I still felt that, with continued hard work, I would eventually master the art, but Fidel Castro had other ideas. After the closing of the university, I transferred to the School of Architecture at the University of Havana. The small classes I was used to were replaced by auditorium-size venues attended by what looked more like fans in a football game than students poised to learn.

The University of Havana is one of the oldest universities in the Americas, founded in 1728 under the reign of King Phillip V of Spain. The imposing building moved to its current site in 1902 and sat atop a hill. After climbing more than a hundred steps, visitors are welcomed to the university's ample grounds by a grand bronze statue of the alma mater.

University of Havana
(Picture taken by Penny Kielpinski, 2012)

A hub of political activities, the institution protected Fidel Castro's supporters during the early years of the revolution. The University of Havana came to represent the Marxist ideals of Fidel's movement. During my two years in attendance, it was not unusual to be caught amid skirmishes and gunfire. I became adept at jumping under benches to protect my illusion of safety.

Not happy with the educational environment and after just a month as an architecture student, I transferred to the School of Languages. In the meantime, I had become engaged to marry Pedro Pablo Bermúdez, a law student attempting to follow in the footsteps of his successful father. I was in love with love, and our parents were in love with the idea that we were a perfect match. The two families' excitement became a source of encouragement, and we were engaged after a year and a half of courtship.

Pedro Pablo had been immersed in several years of Jesuit preparation but finally decided his vocation was not for the priesthood. I had met him in 1957, right after he made the decision to join the lay world. Both sets of parents were elated, entertaining hopes of a possible match. The young man was handsome and gifted, with a great talent to entertain. He could sing. He could imitate any politician or other celebrities, generally becoming the center of attention at every gathering. One thing absent from his abilities was dancing. What bad luck that I would eventually marry the only Cuban who could not dance!

Prior to January 1, 1959, when dictator Fulgencio Batista and members of his government left the island, Cuba had become an unsafe place to live. Violence in the streets, unexpected soft target attacks in public venues, and protests created a climate of instability and fear. Although the revolution was being fought mainly in the Sierra Maestra, the easternmost part of Cuba, Havana was enveloped in rumor and uncertainty. We continued to live our lives, but there was not much appetite for festivity. We lived dreading that something ominous was about to happen.

It did. On January 1, 1959, Fidel Castro was in charge, and our saga to leave the country began. Although, it was evident from its beginnings that Fidel and his loyalists were Marxist-Leninists, Castro denied the connection until much later to ensure acceptance by the Cuban people. When I became engaged to marry, we immediately started plans to make the United States our future home. The day after the wedding ceremony, we left for Varadero Beach for a brief honeymoon. We walked down the beach holding hands and bidding farewell to the island we loved so much.

It was hard to feel celebratory when we knew what was ahead for us. Two weeks later, on August 20, 1960, we boarded a turbo propeller from Compañía Cubana de Aviación to our destination. In my mind, I can still look out the round windows and see my family pretending contentment and my Tata, not even able to pretend, looking dejected. The air of sadness was palpable. On the plane, we were crying as we waved goodbye. We were headed to Ft. Lauderdale, Florida, with what was allowed at the time, a round-trip ticket, thirty pounds of clothing, a big dog, and five dollars. It was a strange combination to take on a honeymoon trip.

We were met by Titahaydeé, who had invited us to stay with her family in Coral Gables until we found a place to live. My husband had been offered a job that was to start right away. It paid $350 a month, which did not sound like much. But instinct, not experience, told us we could manage. I knew little about his job offer, only that it was related to the politics of Cuba.

We had a tough introduction to married life, as I was ill prepared to meet the challenges of domestic bliss. I was only nineteen years old, with zero housewife experience. But I was full of determination to learn. I was hoping that the saying "necessity is the mother of invention" would hold true for me. Learning by trial and error might not be the best way, but it got us out of trouble with a few exceptions. My poor husband, for instance, never wore a white shirt again!

Before long, we found a small furnished efficiency in southwest Miami and bought a red and white used Studebaker for $375 from my husband's cousin. Since I had never cooked or cleaned house before, our new beginnings were a daily adventure. In early September, hurricane Donna came knocking—literally. Our front door faced the street, and we could hear the wind trying to tear it down. Fortunately, it failed, and we were spared once again, this time from another category 4 deadly hurricane. The lesson taught us to look for a safer place within the same complex, and we upgraded to an interior one-bedroom apartment. So, if I stated earlier that my married life in exile started with a bang, it was not an exaggeration.

Soon after, I was hospitalized with a kidney stone that brought me much pain and humiliation. Fortunately, I was able to talk to my father in Cuba, who was shocked that the doctors wanted to remove my kidney.

"You have a kidney stone. Leave the hospital right now. Don't let them get near you again."

I followed my dad's orders, carefully pulling all the various tubes connected to my ailing body, and left the premises "against medical advice."

My father's diagnosis from a distance proved to be correct, and my kidney stone passed without further ado. To this day, I live with two healthy kidneys that have not given me any other sign of grief. If all these incidents taken together were a warning sign, I did not get it then. In a short time, a naive teenager became a seasoned, life-tested adult.

My husband's job was a mystery to me, but I chose not to ask questions. I was still operating under the lesson learned back home that knowing too much would put me in danger. I also had plenty on my plate to worry about. Learning basic domestic undertakings such as shopping, cooking, cleaning, and paying bills was an overwhelming challenge that I managed without much grumbling. I found out that success and risk taking are intimately connected, so I dared try new recipes and invent menus with newly found confidence.

In December of that year, Pedro was involved in an auto accident. A few broken ribs kept him hospitalized for a few days. During that time, I found out that he had been training for the Bay of Pigs invasion and that the accident had delayed his departure to a camp in Central America. *"No hay mal que por bien no venga"* (Every cloud has a silver lining). And I had gotten another reprieve.

In the meantime, I learned for the first time that Pedro's job was to train in a CIA-sponsored operation, Operation 40, which would eventually become part of the ill-fated Bay of Pigs invasion.

I finally realized why I had not asked more questions. Instinctively, I knew there was a connection to the invasion, and I also knew I could not handle the truth at the time. I was prepared now and confident that I would be able to manage his absence in the very near future. I learned to enjoy being by myself and set out to explore markets, people, and my new world.

When the time arrived for him to leave on the invasion, I moved in with my in-laws, who had recently arrived. I did not have a driver's license, but we had a car, and I knew how to drive. Brave enough to drive myself to the DMV office license-less, I was ready to take my test. I confess to feeling apprehensive breaking a law so that I could stop breaking it, but I had no other choice.

Unfortunately, I flunked! I was even more apprehensive leaving the premises, afraid the police would stop me, knowing that I was an unlicensed driver. A week later, I showed up again, but this time I was able to parallel park with flying colors. I was so proud of myself, and I felt successful to finally be under the auspices of the law.

A week after Pedro left, I was driving my father-in-law to his errands when, out of the blue, I said, "Don't you wish your son would be home safe and sound when we get back?"

He replied somberly, "Of course! A nice wish, even if we know it isn't true."

An uncertain stillness followed, allowing each of us to grieve in silence.

As luck would have it, there was a smiling soldier in green fatigues standing by the front door when we returned. It was Pedro, with an astonishing story to tell. The invasion had failed, and Operation 40 never left the training camp. Many of my friends lost their lives or became prisoners of war, but we were fortunate not to be among them.

Soon, he was back to his old self, and we managed to move to our own place to resume our lives. Having completed his work with the CIA, Pedro found employment as a taxi driver.

Still in Cuba, my parents were not fully aware of how the Bay of Pigs ordeal was affecting us. They had seen a newspaper article with a picture of a dead combatant that each thought looked like my brother Carlos but decided not to share their grim suspicion with the other. Their son was very much alive but getting ready to join the invasion as a physician. His group never left either. We could not understand why our parents could not stop crying when they finally heard our voices, until they told us what had transpired.

After the Bay of Pigs, the first one to make it to the United States was my youngest brother, Rod. Our apartment was too small, so he went to live with family. Rod went to work as a sacker in a grocery store, in order to finance English classes at the community college. His dream was to eventually pursue a degree in electrical engineering. During one of his visits, he asked me if I could cut his hair to save money. I had never done that. Nor did I have the proper scissors. But I still forged ahead, no pun intended. The more I tried, the worse it got. I finally decided to stop before I got rid of all the hair. He put a cap on and headed straight to the barbershop. Later, Rod said that, upon arriving, and before he could ask for anything, the barber welcomed him with, "Don't worry. I'll fix it."

Father arrived next in June1961, followed by mother and Fernando a few months later. For the first few weeks, Father devoted his time in preparation for his foreign medical board, a licensing examination required for doctors born abroad to practice as physicians in the United States. Despite the fact that his spoken English was not up to par, he passed without effort. He was used to studying medical texts in English and was very familiar with the terminology. My parents and brother were happy with the news that I was expecting my first child and that they could be present at his birth.

The family was finally together, but not whole, since Tata was still in Cuba. Bringing Tata was more of a challenge. She had no documents, so Mother got to work and succeeded in obtaining a birth certificate and a passport. Once at the airport ready to board, my seventy-something second mother was stopped by immigration and sent back home, under suspicion that her documents were not valid. This experience proved too much for her, and Tata passed away soon after, of a broken heart. As hard as this nightmare was for all of us, we had to go on, but my Tata has never been too far from my thoughts.

My father was able to be employed at the Western State Hospital in Staunton, Virginia, as a general practitioner. Brother Carlos, also a physician, was ready to leave his post there to pursue a urology residency at a Georgia University Hospital and had recommended my father. My parents and Fernando settled in a colonial home on the magnificent hospital grounds.

My parents' home in the Western State Hospital Grounds, Staunton, Virginia

I remember it as if it were today, March 3, 1962, the arrival of my firstborn, Peter. I felt there could be no one happier than I, when a healthy and noisy seven-pounder joined our family. I remember leaving the hospital holding my son and thinking, *How can anyone be luckier than I am?* He was hungry and cried for a solid hour, until I was able to prepare his formula since plans to nurse him had not worked. He was the best gift and definitely a major contribution to my steep learning curve.

Peter in Staunton, 1963
This photo entitled "So this is snow" won first prize in 1963 at
a local contest sponsored by Staunton's *News Leader*

I was a very inexperienced mom and had, as a sidekick, my inexperienced mom. *Abuela* (Grandma) was so protective of her grandson that she would move lamps, furniture, anything and everything from his surroundings, so nothing could fall on the crib and hurt him. We were lucky to have Tía Julita, who had mothered seven children and knew every trick in the book. Mother and I learned how hard it was to care for a demanding baby, yet we both felt we were the luckiest mother and grandmother alive.

At this time, Pedro kept odd hours, since his taxi driver duties did not have a fixed schedule. My parents worried that our lifestyle was not conducive to a future and invited us to move to Virginia with them. The invitation was God-sent, and six weeks after Peter's birth, I arrived with him in Staunton to start a new life. Pedro followed a few weeks later and immediately started job hunting. Very soon, he was offered a job at Staunton Military Academy teaching Spanish, and life with Captain Pedro Bermúdez began. These were happy times for the family.

My father and Peter became soul mates. If Peter cried from his crib, *Abuelo* (Grandfather) came to the rescue in a split second. He would pick up the baby and cuddle him to sleep, while singing old lullabies in his very coarse, out-of-tune, loving voice he had used to sing to me as an infant. My mother was enjoying staying home and learning to cook, garden, and sew. A quick learner, she soon graduated as a fine Cuban gourmet.

Every meal was an adventure and nothing tasted the same more than once, as she managed ingredients in her special secret way. They were either replaced, invented, or removed at will. She was the boss in that kitchen. Both Pedro and Fernando started their graduate studies at the University of Virginia in Charlottesville, some forty miles away, crossing the north end of the spectacular Blue Ridge Parkway. There were many fun times in this house.

My last two children, Flori, born in 1963, and E.J., the following year, made their entrance at King's Daughter's Hospital in Staunton. Right before E.J.'s birth, we built a new home nearby at 2393 Cole Avenue. As our first attempt at independence, the modest home felt to us like a palace. It was. Although the yard was not landscaped, it had a gym set and a children's pool for the growing brood. Pictures from this time show three children, all smiles, having fun.

Peter at 2393 Cole Avenue, Staunton, 1964

We added a puppy, Go-go, to the family, only to find out that Flori was absolutely horrified. For the most part, she avoided Go-go by sitting on her legs on the sofa. I felt that the best strategy to resolve the warfare was to ignore it and let them figure out how to get along. It worked. One day, while playing hide-and-seek, Flori came out of a closet giggling, followed by a bouncing Go-go.

In the meantime, my father was invited to practice in the state of Maryland, which opened up an opportunity for him to go into private practice in family medicine. The opportunity could not be passed up, and plans for them to move to Cambridge started at once. By then, Mother was teaching English and Spanish at Riverheads High School in Staunton.

When the Augusta County Public Schools could not find a Spanish teacher to replace her, they offered me an emergency certificate to finish my mother's spring semester. I was ecstatic with the opportunity, and although I had only two years of college and no experience, I took the risk, and so did the school district. The semester went fast, with no issues of concern. On the last day, the deputy superintendent came to visit me in my class to thank me for "my beautiful job." He was apologetic that my contract could not be extended but offered me a full scholarship at Mary Baldwin College, along with the comment "you were born to teach."

Three children under three, a demanding husband, and school kept me busy just trying to keep my head above water, but the thought of a future kept me motivated. Pedro had continued traveling to Charlottesville, and in 1966 he completed his master's degree. He was offered a teaching job at Randolph-Macon Woman's College (now Randolph College), a leading Virginia institution of higher education in Lynchburg. The contract included a full scholarship for me to continue my undergraduate studies. Accepting the offer was a no-brainer, so we soon moved to 2209 Rivermont Avenue in Lynchburg.

Flori, Peter and E.J. in 2209 Rivermont Avenue, Lynchburg

The next two years provided our family with lots of possibilities. The children had adapted well to life in Lynchburg. They attended kindergarten and preschool respectively, learned English, and made their first friends. I carpooled everyone to school, including my husband and then, after straightening up the house, drove myself to class. I was alive, inspired by my new busy life with zero chance for boredom.

Our lives left very little opportunities to socialize, so I was still feeling like a visitor to the country. I had to make time to experience life beyond school and home, to learn know how to deal with life in the new culture. I graduated in 1968 with honors, and Pedro had attained the "all but dissertation" status in his PhD. The next step was to continue our academic journey at the University of Virginia, in Charlottesville. I was accepted to pursue a master's degree, and we were both offered teaching assistantships. Now, it was time to move again, and the family was ready for Charlottesville.

A three-bedroom student apartment not too far from campus became our new home. We were pleased with the options for the children's first grade, kindergarten, and pre-primary, so we were set. I so enjoyed this year in Charlottesville. Teaching first-year Spanish was my greatest challenge, as there is a big difference between the language one acquires as a native speaker and the second language my students had to learn. Some rules were new to me, and I had to become aware of what were the challenging grammatical issues for my English-speaking students. I had to study and prepare for my classes, since I thought "just because" would be an inappropriate answer to my students', "Why?"

I established a great rapport with my all-male, mostly Virginia "gentlemen." My husband and I made time to party with our classmates, which added a dimension we had missed before, and the year seemed to have flown by. On August 20, 1969, we graduated from UVA. Despite the success in moving forward in our lives, our personal relationship had not survived that well.

When Pedro was offered a job at the University of Houston in Texas, I saw it as an opportunity to end the marriage. My brother Fernando intervened, warning me of the challenges of single motherhood. I decided to give another chance to our marriage, considering the children's well-being this time. The new job paid $12,000 a year, which sounded to us like a fortune, since our individual income the year before had been $1,500. I soon found part-time work at a couple of private universities in Houston, Rice and St. Thomas, and we settled into our new environment.

We bought a modest home in 1970 at 5330 Darnell, in the middle-class neighborhood of Meyerland. The children were delighted with the large patio and the many neighborhood friends they were making. This step marked the end of an era, my twenties, when change, adaptation, and growth helped me travel through the challenging adventures and prepared me for what was to come.

PART III

OUR NEW WORLD

CHAPTER 9

ADAPTING TO LIFE IN EXILE

S ince my immediate family left Cuba in installments, it took us two years to reunite in the United States. It would be untrue to say we "never looked back." Although all of us considered ourselves lucky to immigrate to the United States, I still longed for the island, for my family being together, for my loyal Tata, and for my lost friends. I waited until my yearning became a memory to pursue citizenship in a country that had received me with open arms and given me an opportunity for a fresh start.

The painful memory of a lost homeland has never gone away, but an appreciation for freedom has made the new beginning a more satisfying experience. Freedom of speech, freedom of thought, and freedom of action were lost forever after the arrival of Communism to the island, and escaping this fate meant seeking refuge in places where freedom was respected. Fortunately, the United States was our choice, and giving up our homeland was the price of being free.

The "American Dream"

I spent my first nineteen years in a culture that forged the foundation for my beliefs. When I left, I was ill equipped to face the next step in my journey, exile. Leaving oppression and hopelessness behind, we chose freedom and opportunity in a new and different land. Some call this opportunity, the pursuit of the "American dream," not necessarily a fallacy but indeed a misnomer. A better term would be the "American prospect," as the country offers opportunities for advancement without guarantee of rewards. Achieving the American dream is entirely dependent on the efforts of those who dream the dream, whose luck, skills, and hard work will make it happen.

Beyond learning the language and becoming adept in the culture, the newly arrived has to endure a pervasive anti-immigrant disdain in order to achieve the dream. Racism is rampant, and being different, having darker skin, or sporting an "accent" becomes the target of prejudice. It does not matter that the United States is, indeed, a tapestry of expatriates.

The struggle for belonging in the culture never stops, until the recently arrived reach the status of "old" immigrants. In most cases, that is a sign that the immigrant has managed to adapt. Some become fully assimilated, an option not opened to the nonwhites, who can still accommodate to the new value system, customs, and language without giving up who they truly are. They cannot meld with the mainstream, but they can definitely function successfully in the new environment.

Different standards are applied to people from other countries, and they generally become second class in the already established hierarchy. Calling these people "diverse" or believing they have an "accent" indicates that the mainstream is the gold standard. If we use ourselves as the norm, everyone is diverse, and everyone has an accent. I experimented with my students, mostly monolingual English speakers from all over the United States, and asked who among them had an accent. Texans swore they did not have one, but believed New Yorkers did and vice versa. We all learned that having an accent is not a negative, as it is merely a reflection of one's roots, and as such, it is a badge of honor.

Adapting to the New Culture

Immigrants face many cultural challenges in adjusting to the way of life of their adoptive country. Learning a new language may sound easy to those who have never tried. We hear often enough, "Why don't they learn English? We're in the United States," as if referring to something as easy as tying your shoes. It does not matter how long you have been in the country or how well you have mastered English, there are times when you struggle in vain with its complexities. For instance, becoming skilled in the use of English prepositions is a challenging task, very difficult to master if you are not a native speaker.

Recently, we had a wedding to attend. When given directions, I understood the celebration was to take place "in Galisteo," a town about twenty-five miles from our home. My partner, Deb, prepared for the long trek, fed the puppies, filled the gas tank, and turned on a light in case we were late returning. After all the arrangements, we discovered that the ceremony was to be held "on Galisteo," a street just a couple of miles away—a small mistake with far-reaching consequences! The funny thing is that my Cuban American friend María, in a separate exchange, had understood the same thing I had.

An issue monolingual speakers don't fully realize is that words are meaningless, unless we understand the values and mores of the culture. Time and space, what, how, and when to say something, are not universal constructs, and yet they rule effective communication. Take this exchange, for example, between Mrs. López and Mr. García as they discuss directions to a friend's house:

Mr. García. Where does Jimmy live?

Mrs. López. Go up two or three blocks; I am not sure. There is either a light or a stop sign, but right there you can see the pink house where the Ortegas live.

Mr. García. Oh, the Ortegas live there? I did not know. You know their daughter is having a baby.

Mrs. López. She is? I am happy for them. She is so young, but I hear the husband is really nice.

Mr. García. Yes, he is. They are very happy.

Mrs. López. At any rate, turn left on that street. You will see a bunch of houses, and Jimmy's is the one with the big tree in front.

Mr. Garcia. Thanks.

How would you rate this exchange? If you are a monolingual English speaker, assimilated to the mainstream culture, you may find it annoying, maybe even a waste. You were looking for information, and that is the least you received. If you understand that cultures and languages have different purposes, you may give your low ratings a second look. Whether you generally use language to inform or to entertain can become a source of miscommunication across cultures.

I also learned from these experiences that we all live in multiple realities, but we tend to equate "real" with truth. There is no single reality, only perspectives. We look at the "real world" through the prism of our culture. Adaptation to a new medium requires that we do not take for granted that what we say or do will be interpreted the way we meant it. Becoming aware of the filters we use in interpreting cultural situations is quite a sophisticated skill that takes time to acquire. Not doing so will be the source of great misunderstandings. A person could be considered "loud" in one culture, while being perfectly acceptable to another. Being able to read the tea leaves and decide which words or actions are appropriate requires knowledge and respect for the customs and values of the new environment.

Spanish is my native tongue, so I speak English with a slight "accent." I have been asked if I am Italian or even German but, ironically, never British. Although some people call it charming, it can sometimes get you in a bit of trouble. While doing my daily walk, I ran into a neighbor I didn't know with her adorable puppy. The little one, the puppy, wanted to greet me, and I proceeded to tell the lady that I had two miniature dachshunds at home. She looked at me funny, and I knew then that she thought I was talking about the Japanese cars. From now on, I shall drop the proper name and call them "winnies." Thinking about it, this may be worse.

Being intentional in what you say or do is important, but being understood in your intentions is a necessary condition to communicate and succeed in the new environment. When individuals fail to adapt, they become marginalized, with few options for upper mobility. People face innumerable challenges in trying to interact across cultures. Generally, learning to deal with life requires a modicum of adaptation to change. In my case, the rules I had mastered were no longer viable, so I had to figure out what worked now. Unfortunately, it is not until you make mistakes that you learn lessons in what needs to change to make a successful transition to the new culture.

My first mistake was made trying to make friends in the United States. For me, the joy of friendship has always been an important element in my life, but understanding how to make friends in the new culture was not an easy accomplishment. I was used to treating friends as an extension of myself, and I did not realize that my views were overstepping the social boundaries of my new world.

The idea of "needing space" was totally alien to me, so it took me a while to understand that, although friendships are also important in the United States, allowing our friends their own space was necessary to maintain thriving relationships. After many years, I have come to appreciate what "space" means to me, in terms of personal enrichment. Becoming a whole person should not depend on others, but on building resources that make us feel accomplished. The presence of others should be, instead, icing on the cake.

I count as a blessing having had the ability to learn new ways of communicating through language and actions without giving up who I am. I am proud of my heritage, and I am constantly aware that I am its voice. As a representative of a people, I realize that it is only when my message is understood as intended that the voice is truly heard. This only happens when we become aware of how our message is perceived and learn to modify our behaviors accordingly. Easy to say, much harder to do!

Understanding the New Culture

My parents were well educated and had a strong belief that their children would succeed if they followed that path. While still living in Cuba, my mother insisted that I attend American schools, where I would be taught English at an early age. She loved the language, and as a challenge to the mores of her generation, she received her advanced degree in English. During my elementary grades, at the Dominican school, kindergarten offered me the first opportunity to study English. I learned to read with Dick, Jane, and Spot. I could follow some of the dialogue but often thought their games were strange. It was also alien to see Dick and Jane playing together all the time, while in my culture gender segregation was generally the rule.

My high school years at Ruston Academy became my salvation, as the experience gave me a profound exposure to the culture and language of the United States. I remember how, at first, the lessons learned in senior English were so meaningless. In class, we were reading about the "rat race" and about the "survival of the fittest," while living in a culture where community was more important than individual undertakings, and competition was not a factor to be considered. Besides improving my English language skills, I learned important cultural lessons about competition, winning, and survival—three fundamentals of my future life in exile.

The new Ruston building in the Biltmore neighborhood, circa 1956

Mother's love of English was probably responsible for my year abroad in 1954. Being in Washington, DC, for a whole academic year allowed me the opportunity for immersion in the language and culture of the country. Living in community with native speakers gave me the perspective I needed to not only gain greater fluency in the language, but also develop an understanding of American values and preferences. So, fortunately for us, we started our life in exile with the gift of language, thanks to Mother's visionary insistence that we become fluent in English.

I became aware that native speakers of English don't necessarily have to learn all the rules and regulations before they speak, since they acquire language by listening to adult speakers around them. In a similar fashion, they acquire their cultural patterns by observing, imitating, and interacting with their environment. This is why many native English speakers are not able to explain what rules apply, why they behave in certain ways, or even how certain words are spelled. In contrast, second language learners are taught rules, spelling, and vocabulary, including vernacular phrases whose meaning is not literal and, as a result, need to be memorized.

These expressions are frequent in communication and are responsible for many unsuccessful but mostly humorous exchanges. In addition, knowing what is acceptable and what is not must be considered, as these cultural features grant meaning to our words. At the hospital one morning, my father was answering a phone call from one of his nurses. When she was done with the conversation, she asked my dad to "hang on."

He thought he understood, so he placed the phone on its cradle. A few minutes later, his nurse came running and laughing. She patiently explained to him what "hang on" meant. A while later, there was another call from the same nurse, who, this time, told Dad, "Okay, Doc, now you can hang up." My dad, proud that he remembered the explanation, remained on the line, while the nurse continued to say, "Hang up, hang up." He finally caught on, not without feeling a bit stupid!

Those of us who have gone through the process of learning the grammatical backbone of English have our work cut out for us when we try to apply the rules to a conversation. For one thing, inconsistencies abound. One learns that "in" means inside and "on" on top, only to get on the plane! Try knowing what to do with tow, cow, mow, bow, and bow. In addition, as discussed earlier, learning the do's and don'ts in the new culture is a monumental task in itself. Values and behavioral rules are not universal, as people decide within their borders what is best for them.

Unfortunately, there are no written manuals of behavior, and the only way to learn is by confronting situations head-on and judging success by what results follow. Take simple gestures, for instance. The act of saying "goodbye" and "come here" are reversed in the United States and in Cuba. That caused a bit of misunderstanding between Mother and a plumber, whom she was trying to call back as he was leaving the house. She noticed that, in response to her gesture, he kept leaving waving back at her, until she realized her mistake. Mother was a bit embarrassed, wondering if he thought she was nuts.

Adapting to a different culture does not mean giving up who you are or what preferences you have but, rather, learning to respond to situations in ways that aren't offensive to the native culture. Being able to function in both worlds calls for a deep understanding of and respect for the people and their value system. The process cannot be completed in seven days. Only God can do that.

CHAPTER 10

TAKING STOCK: MY LIFE ACCOMPLISHMENTS

I often wonder if my accomplishments have been happenstance or the result of overcoming the many challenges I have encountered in my adventurous journey. It wasn't an easy road to travel in my youth, as then it seemed that I had to fight those around me to claim my place. I have always been different from others, the youngest in my class, late to develop, hyperactive, attention deficit, and probably too smart for my own good. These traits made me live the life of a child misunderstood.

In trying to fit in, I closed my eyes to what made me different and proceeded to do what was accepted by society. Moving to the United States gave me an opportunity to fight the status quo, search for the unique qualities that made me the person I am today, and have the courage to be myself.

Personal Accomplishments

Although I am not one to let any of my accomplishments go to my head, I feel successful. To me success happens when you hear an opportunity knocking and you open that door. I do not like to compare my "successes" with someone else's, as I think we are all born with gifts, as well as limitations, that set off how we function, the choices we make, and the results we attain. Doing our best with the cards dealt to us is my definition of accomplishment. Complaining or wishing things were different are distractions that keep us from doing our best and from achieving our intended goals.

Developing self-confidence was a difficult accomplishment during my childhood and early adulthood in Cuba, where children, especially females grew up under the constant vigilance of an adult. Cuban girls had the responsibility of representing the family name, resulting in older members zealously protecting them. Not being allowed to fail because an adult was there to "save" me made it nearly impossible to gauge what abilities, determination, or courage I possessed. So, if I had to evaluate my self-confidence at that time in my life, I would place it close to zero on a scale of one to ten. Most likely, I would not have known the term, since it had never been put to a test.

I had to become an adult in a hurry, having left my country of birth so young to start my new life, accompanied by an inexperienced husband and the pet German shepherd. The transition from a protected cocoon to real life on my own happened in the forty-five minutes that it took to fly from Havana to Ft. Lauderdale.

Sink or swim it was, and swimming upstream I did with a modicum of success. I consider an early personal achievement in exile the first meal I attempted to cook. I took out a hand embroidered tablecloth I had brought from Cuba, lit a few candles, and placed a bouquet of beautiful wild flowers at the center of our modest dining room table. I had been working all day on a chicken recipe from my Tía Julita, to be served over white rice.

Everything looked phenomenal to me, and I was feeling a bit full of myself. When my husband sat at the dining table, he seemed pretty impressed with the atmosphere I had created. The first words out of his mouth worried me, "Great chicken. Wow, stuffed!" My balloon popped! I had not stuffed the chicken. I had just failed to remove the plastic pouch containing its insides. We laughed, and I learned. This was the beginning of my trial to develop domestic skills and responsibilities. As time passed, failures and successes became the foundation for building trust in myself as I approached new experiences on a daily basis.

When reflecting upon my upbringing, I realize that having been overprotected had hindered my ability to develop survival skills. I needed to break that chain to help my children develop their self-confidence. I realized that I would have to let them learn from their own mistakes with minimal intervention on my part, other than offering support or guidance when necessary. Life was showing me that trusting the young to make their own decisions, allowing them to fail, to succeed, and to learn, is the most beneficial way to help them meet their future successfully.

In looking back, I am astounded to think of the many mountains I have climbed, feeling that I have conquered the unbeatable. Beyond self-confidence, courage and determination have also been contributing factors in my successful climb. I am a survivor because I have not feared taking risks and have learned from both failure and success. In other words, *"no le tengo miedo al susto,"* which in figurative terms means, "I am not afraid of fear."

At this time in my life, I protect my sanity by respecting my need for organization, order, and focus. I am not ruled by the calendar, but I allow it to help me travel through the day, fulfill commitments, and most importantly not miss any pleasurable moments. Being an undiagnosed attention deficit disorder individual, I have a serious need to pay attention to one thing at a time. I do not let my mind wander, except when I need to be creative, plan, or solve a problem. I add to my list of accomplishments having learned to concentrate and enjoy the moment.

Wearing the Many Hats of Single Motherhood

My three children woke up to reality early in their lives, when I decided to divorce their father after twelve years of marriage. Realizing that, together, we would not get much farther, I took my story to an attorney in 1972. And a year later, our separation was final. My parents finally accepted that the divorce was my decision to make and that I had dreams and plans for a brighter time ahead.

Single motherhood, complicated by a triad of part-time jobs while attending school, left just enough room to breathe. The reward was the three children who, for the most part, cooperated by not getting into any serious trouble. Aside from minor skirmishes, mostly from E.J. (tempting hurricanes, an arsenal of *Playboy* magazines under the bed, and an assortment of derelict cars that had to be towed home), life went on unperturbed. We had a savior in Father James Gaunt, principal of the boys' school, who was always on call in case of an emergency.

Tempting hurricanes became the boys' favorite pastime. They would join friends, and go to Galveston to enjoy a day of surfing. I did not find this out until later years, when it was safe for Mom to discover the dangers they had invited. Adventure was E.J.'s center of gravity, his core. For the most part, he was always caught red-handed, if his escapade went awry. Years later, I had an adult chat with Peter, who was always the voice of reason; he assured me that he had done everything E.J. had, except that I had never caught him in the act. I was thankful to E.J.'s guardian angel for having worked so hard to keep him safe.

E.J. in Galveston, Texas

The day I found the stack of *Playboy* magazines under fourteen-year-old E.J.'s bed, I must confess, I panicked. Father Gaunt responded in his usual calmness and persuaded me that this find was part of growing up. I was advised not to make a big deal about it. "When he notices that you have removed the magazines, he will be embarrassed and regret the whole thing. That should put an end to the story. I will have a chat with him later on."

I did as I was told, double bagging the magazines and placing them in the trash bin. The three children left for school; I took the trash out and left for work.

To my utter embarrassment, when I returned home, I saw on the pavement a page from the magazine. It must have been one of E.J.'s favorites, but there it was. I was furious. I picked it up and waited for the perpetrator. When he came home, I just grabbed the page and gave it to him. "Here is your butt. Get rid of it."

We both burst out laughing and hugged.

The next day, a very contrite young man apologized. It never happened again.

Part of Father Gaunt's approach to disciplining the boys was to take them to work on cars during weekends and use the opportunity to give them advice and guidance. He would take old cars and transform them into safe vehicles that the boys could use. I don't know how many E.J. drove, but it was not uncommon to get a call from him that his "free" vehicle had stalled. In time, he learned to be an incredible mechanic. Today, there is nothing he can't fix, having become the penultimate honey do.

Flori loved her friends and parties but never overstepped any boundaries. Her room could be an example of orderliness, or a total disaster depending on how she felt that day. She was responsible at home, and was always able to keep a part-time job. I went to the hospital for a few days, and I still get choked up when I remember the children's visit. There was Flori, dressed in a pretty blue dress, accompanied by E.J., and carrying a bouquet of flowers she had bought with money she had saved. On another occasion, she was so excited about her high school graduation that she wore her red gown all day on the eve of her commencement, even while helping me paint the living room. There was a drop of paint on her gown as a reminder.

Peter was the perfectionist. Half the boys' room reflected this trait. He was the embodiment of his great-grandmother Barroso's favorite quote: *"Un lugar para cada cosa y cada cosa en su lugar"* (a place for everything and everything in its place.) I remember passing his first job site and seeing him with a broom cleaning the patio. He waved and smiled with the pride of being at work. He was generous to a fault and enjoyed gifting the family with his hard-earned money.

During the summers, my parents would take the children to Maryland so I could attend summer school. Their father had moved to Argentina with his new family, so he was mostly absent during their growing-up years. In summer 1975, my parents took all three children on a trip to Europe that was to be my mother's last. They had an unforgettable experience, which was recorded by E.J. in a small yellow notebook. My father told me that the travel guides would invite E.J. to the front of the group, so he could hear well and take his profuse notes.

My life was not my own then. I was absorbed in somebody else's world. At home, I was a mother of three; at school, a student following a professor's guidance; and at work, I was a teacher, intent on providing opportunities for my students to seek and discover. There was no space that was my own and no part of me I could claim for myself. Once Peter left for the University of Texas in 1980, I realized one of my roles in life was about to be concluded. The offspring were leaving the nest in pursuit of their life purpose.

I had to find out what mine was beyond motherhood. I had no hobbies or interests, although I had always believed sanity depends on them. I had to search for my identity, and this was the opportune time.

In 1982, Peter's death in a car accident shook us to the very core. We had taken for granted our family unit, and it was no longer. Anger invaded us. Why Peter? We never got an answer but had to go on living without it. There wasn't a thing we could humanly do to reset the clock. No one could help us now, and we had to find strength and courage from within. Miracles do happen, when we need them, and the three of us were able to survive. The pain of his loss never left us, but his wonderful memories managed to sooth our grieving hearts.

I often wondered if I had sacrificed my youth for my children or if my staying so busy had been an act of selfishness. When I see what great parents they have become, I can't help but take a little credit for it. My children must have realized what I had given up and understood that my sacrifice had been for them.

Professional Accomplishments

My mother's example was the driving force behind my attaining higher education. Very soon into my marriage, I realized that my ex, although Jesuit-educated, lacked a sense of future. Tired of wanting and full of desire to improve our circumstances, I pursued my plans to build a better future for my children.

When I left Cuba, I had completed two years at the University of Havana, but I had too many disruptions to even think of going back to school during the first few years of life in exile. As discussed earlier, life is full of surprises, so when my mother decided to join Father in Maryland, I inherited her job. It had been quite an experience to be a stay-at-home mom, but it was time for me to help the family build a future.

I remember teaching football players who tried to get away with their popularity and local fame. I ultimately earned their respect and was rewarded with much improved behavior. I also remember participating in a talent show as Paul McCartney dubbing the Beatles' "I Want to Hold Your Hand." It was a moment of *déjà vu* all over again. I was duplicating an earlier success in elementary school circa 1949, when I dubbed Al Jolson.

A similar temporary fame and popularity followed my performance. Both students and peers found it hysterical that a Cuban would successfully portray a British icon! A picture of the event appeared in the yearbook, making the moment live forever. I was experiencing American life for the first time, and thriving as a person and a professional.

I recall how determined I was to pursue my education, particularly in light of receiving scholarships to complete my undergraduate degree. The challenge of three children so close in age was intimidating, but not enough to discourage me from continuing my studies. The joy of graduating in the spring of 1968 is still felt. Surrounded by my tots, family and friends, I felt on top of the world, and now I knew, for a fact, that nothing could stop me. The teaching assistantship offered by the University of Virginia was further motivation. I loved the challenge of my graduate classes and of teaching beginning Spanish to an all-male student audience who came to class in suits and ties.

Attending college and, later, the Universities of Virginia and Houston for my graduate studies fueled my need to get ahead. After graduation in 1969 from the University of Virginia, we moved to Houston, Texas, where we found employment at various universities. Armed with my master's degree in Spanish literature and linguistics, I joined the University of St. Thomas and Rice University as a part-time instructor. I realized very soon that I needed a doctorate to be able to advance in my profession, but was disappointed that in a major city as large as Houston, there were no PhD programs offered in my chosen field of Spanish literature.

Driving four hours a week in each direction to the University of Texas in Austin was not feasible with three young children, ages seven to nine. I settled for a doctorate in education from the University of Houston, a degree that served me well throughout my long career as an educator. I became Dr. Bermúdez in summer 1974, a year after my divorce was final but in time to still make my mother proud.

It was on October 12, 1971, that I received my United States citizenship. The fact that it took eleven years after my arrival had nothing to do with the length of the process. I wanted to wait until my heart was ready to embrace the new country as my own. I wanted to feel American, and to be in command of the culture and the language. On that date and beyond, I stopped being an observer of the culture and became an active participant.

I eventually went to work at the University of Houston-Clear Lake, where I was offered many opportunities to grow and serve thousands of students. In the early 1990s, I was selected to participate in a pilot program using television as a distance education venue. The program was a partnership among a TV network, the state education agency, and my university. It was exciting to be a part of a future that promised to extend education beyond institutional walls.

The catch was that the class had to be transmitted from a studio in San Antonio, Texas, an hour away by plane. Every Monday, I would fly to my class in the morning, and return home late that night, ready for a more traditional rest of the week. For a professor, this unique form of transportation added to the already challenging circumstances.

As a TV instructor, I was operating from a small room with a desk, an overhead projector, and the red eye of a camera staring at me throughout the class. The desk had all the necessary instrumentation to select camera angle, adjust the sound, share my materials on the projector, and still keep track of the information I was attempting to deliver. I felt like a newly minted engineer. The experience put my ability to multitask to a test.

My students were attending in small groups at educational service centers spread around several cities in the state. They could hear and see me, but I could only hear them. I learned their names and composed pictures of how they must have looked, as I wanted to establish a more "personalized" approach. Class only worked well when the weather was good. Storms, a frequent event in any of these cities, would interrupt transmission, so once reconnected, I had to backtrack to make sure all my students would receive the same information.

The experiment was successful, albeit expensive, and served to pave the way for the world of online learning at my institution. Technology evolves at a rapid speed, so being a part of this world required constant retraining and dedication to change. After the exciting experience, I decided to continue my teaching career on-site, face-to-face, as I felt more rewarded with the personal interactions.

By the time I retired, a distance education department had been added, and it had been my responsibility, as an associate provost, to supervise it. My years at the University of Houston-Clear Lake were exciting and productive. I started in 1980 as an instructor and progressed through the ranks until my retirement in 2003 as an emerita professor. During ten years of my twenty-five-year tenure, I had brought several millions of dollars in Title VII grants that supported the education of hundreds of teachers and public school administrators in our area. It also supported the creation of the Research Center for Language and Culture and the first Apple computer lab at the university.

A very interesting event happened during those years that prove that destiny is an important determinant in facilitating or limiting our accomplishments. A colleague and I were invited to present one of our studies at the American Educational Research Association (AERA), a highly respected scholarly organization. My friend was a statistician, so we had developed a study together regarding second language acquisition, my specialty. As our names were called, she informed me, "It would look strange for both of us to present the paper," and urged me to go ahead and do it solo. She promised that, if any questions on the statistical end would emerge, she would back me up. I had no time to panic, so armed with composure (*cara dura*), I stood up and turned on my charm.

I must say, it went flawlessly, and no nitpicking questions were asked, so my friend never had to come to my rescue. As we were prepared to exit the session, a smiling short lady approached me and said the magic words that set me up for life, "I am a textbook editor searching for an author in second language learning, and I liked what I heard."

The conversation fueled several years of association with her textbook company, and a series of language arts books grades six to twelve were produced. My colleague never knew how much it cost her to relinquish an opportunity due to fear.

After my first retirement in 2003, I was hired by Santa Fe Community College as a vice president for Academic and Student Affairs. I wanted to complete my understanding of the American educational system, and experiencing the role of community colleges seemed like an exciting challenge. Being able to combine living in beautiful Santa Fe, New Mexico, with my professional life seemed like a grand idea, and I was delighted to accept the new task.

I found community colleges to be where the action is in education. Their primary focus is to prepare the workforce, so these institutions serve students who are not necessarily inclined to continue to a four-year degree and beyond. I found the staff and faculty to be very dedicated to their work, and I greatly appreciated my association with them. I was not as impressed with the administration. I found that a place as small as the college did not warrant a bureaucratic, top-heavy, and stagnant leadership.

After two years, I was happy to accept a position at Miami Dade College (MDC) in Florida. The college is the largest in the United States and serves over a quarter of a million students on several campuses throughout South Florida. My job was to lead academic affairs at the Kendall campus.

Beyond the professional responsibility, the offer also allowed me an opportunity to reconnect with my Cuban roots. Soon, I was being treated to a *colada* (enough espresso coffee for five people), a ritual that happened every morning around ten. The first time it was offered, I did not realize that the small paper cups it came with were meant for other people, and drank the whole thing. My Puerto Rican secretary, Peter Dávila, was amused and reminded me that I had been gone too long.

At the Kendall Campus during my welcome reception, 2005

Despite my professional and personal satisfaction at MDC, I was ready for my next step, a third and final retirement. The picture of a life reveling in my grandchildren, having time for myself, and enjoying opportunities to travel and write, finally convinced me that I had come full circle.

I feel that I have experienced the American dream. I have worked hard, sacrificed my youth, and been rewarded with a respectable life. I have found out that the American dream does exist, but it does not land on your lap like a butterfly. Achieving its promise requires work, commitment, constant learning, and the ability to change without compromising your true nature.

PART IV

TOOLS FOR A HAPPY JOURNEY

CHAPTER 11

BUILDING COMMUNITY

Many survive the perils of one's journey, but thriving under challenging conditions requires interactions and community. My support system has increased my knowledge of life, nurtured courage and determination to live a meaningful existence, and amplified my enjoyment of the moment. Support systems are idiosyncratic, so they need to be self-defined to match the exclusive needs of each individual. These systems generally involve friends, meaningful activities, pets, or family, all serving the common purpose of helping to endure hard times.

Opening up to others has definitely enhanced my journey. There are many wonderful people involved in my life today. My partner, Deb; members of my family; friends; and memories of dear friends play a critical role in making my life more consequential and enjoyable. Deb has been in my life for the past fifteen years. She has been my rock, supporting me at every turn. Whether I am right or wrong, Deb is always on my side. She prefers the simple life, devoid of superfluous possessions, and makes giving to others the centerpiece of her life.

Generous to a fault, her greatest joy as a child was to save her allowance so she could treat her little friends at the neighborhood convenience store. This trait has developed through the years. There is a happy street newspaper vendor in Santa Fe, who beams at the sight of Deb's car, because he gets to keep the change from a ten or a twenty! I have learned from her to be more responsible about our physical surroundings and more respectful of creatures that, in her own words, make Mother Nature her God and the wilderness her church.

Role of the Children and Grandchildren in My Support System

My oldest child, Peter, was a month and ten days old on my twenty-first birthday in 1962. I had never babysat or even taken lessons on how to care for a baby, so Peter had to be patient, while his mom was learning on the job. I was the happiest young mom on the planet, undoubtedly feeling the privilege of motherhood. Peter and I grew up together, and he survived my learning curve. A cutup, he was always looking for the opportunity to entertain, which he did with relish. He grew up to be a perfectionist, trying in vain to keep his little brother organized. Their room told the story—one half had the bed made, and everything in place, the other half ... well.

Handsome and funny, Peter was a popular teenager. He loved his many friends, especially prankster Ricky Gutiérrez. They were inseparable. Beyond his many outward gifts was Peter's generous spirit. With meager earnings from a first job, he bought the family expensive gifts to mark birthdays and holidays. To this day, I treasure a brand-name cooking pan he gave me, aptly named Peter Pan, one of my most favorite possessions.

Showcasing Peter's penchant for clowning, 1964

Peter was a good student and a gifted athlete, especially in track and field. I still remember his first, and maybe only, touchdown, when this skinny twelve-year-old outran his Blue Devils' football opponents.

With enormous grief for the family, Peter's life was cut short on August 14, 1982, in a car accident while visiting my father in Maryland. Peter lived his life with gusto, and despite his youth, he made a difference in the lives of many.

Florinda María (Flori) was born on October 29, 1963, two days after a head-on collision that fortunately did not injure anyone involved. When the ambulance arrived at the scene of the accident, the EMTs wanted to give me a ride, since I looked ready for motherhood. I declined but volunteered my shaken mother-in-law to be transported. She refused as well. All in all, we were fine.

Flori was born in Staunton, Virginia, a healthy baby with no signs of trauma and a beautiful head of jet-black hair. In those days, it was customary to spend a week hospitalized after labor. So every morning, rookie mothers would receive training in baby care. They used Flori as the model, and I assumed it was because, to my eyes, she was perfect. I remember how good it felt to receive kudos from the other, mostly green-with-envy, moms.

Flori was a beautiful baby, and as the months passed, the jet-black hair turned blond and her eyes as blue as sapphires. Big brother Peter took well to the competition of a baby sister and modified his energetic ways to show tenderness toward her.

Many years later while in elementary school at Holy Ghost, she showed talent as a painter. Once, during a parent-teacher conference, I was captivated by a beautiful acrylic of Hansel and Gretel adorning the classroom. I was taken aback to hear it was Flori's. She had not shown any interest in painting at home before, so we were not aware we had talented artist in our midst.

Flori and E.J. in 1977

Flori had many friends and boyfriends. But a special one caught her heart, a dairy farmer named James Oross. They had met while she was visiting my father in Maryland. After two years of dating, they decided a big wedding was not for them, so they called to tell me they had just become Mr. and Mrs. Oross. The happy couple had opted for the simple life. James and Flori built a home on the family farm and have been married for over twenty years. Their children, John Paul and Katherine, have grown up to make their parents and grandparents proud.

Eleven months and thirteen days after Flori's birth, Evelio Joseph arrived on October 13, 1964. His beautiful old family name did not survive the short hospital stay, as he was renamed E.J. by the hospital nurses. Early on, I knew this boy would be the family's entertainer. Gifted with an adult sense of humor, E.J. soon learned how to wiggle out of trouble. I remember spending an inordinate amount of time refinishing a coffee table, only to later find E.J.'s handprint on it. When confronted, he simply said, "See, Mom, now you will always remember me." I don't know how many times I heard from him, "Well, Mom, nobody is perfect." As if.

Brett Schneider was E.J.'s best friend. Of about the same age, they shared a similar desire to challenge the world's norms. The boys were inseparable, and together they managed to survive their insatiable appetite for adventure. When Hurricane Alicia visited Houston, E.J. and

Brett built a raft to ride the Chimney Rock Bayou in Houston. To say it was a miracle that they were able to tell the story is an understatement.

On another occasion, when the pair was returning home, they noticed a strange car running suspiciously slowly, as if the driver were focusing on them. Armed with good survival instincts, the boys jumped over a neighbor's fence and ran from backyard to backyard until they got home safely. Days later, a young neighbor was abducted by Elmer Wayne Henley, a serial killer, who was eventually apprehended in 1974. It was our boys' full-time guardian angel who came to their rescue one more time.

E.J. and I at his graduation from St. Thomas High School, Class of '81

E.J. grew up to be a responsible family man. He married Julie Vitello, and they are the parents of four amazing children, Julianne, Peter, Andrea, and Max. Flori and E.J. lead their lives independently, caring for their wonderful children and making sure their future is secure. Flori and James live on their dairy farm, which requires that James work from dawn to dusk. Julie, E.J.'s wife, has become more a daughter than an in-law. We have developed a very healthy relationship, in which I do not act as a "know-it-all-tell-her-what-to do" mother in-law. I have come to understand that unwanted advice is useless for many reasons—one of them being that the experience of the younger generation is not necessarily a good fit with advice shaped by a very dissimilar set of experiences.

My greatest personal accomplishment in life, however, is the grand-children, mainly because that means I survived their parents. There are six children in this world that call me Nani—John Paul, Katherine, Julianne, Peter, Andrea, and Max. What a privilege! Unfortunately, they don't live close to me geographically, but they are never far from my thoughts.

Galveston, Texas, 2010
From left to right: Kat, Julianne, Peter, Andrea, Max, and John Paul

My eldest grandson, John Paul, is in college pursuing a master's de-gree in history with a minor in education. He is tall and lanky, and his face sports a beard to remind me that time has passed since this beautiful baby boy with golden hair and blue eyes made me a grandmother for the first time. The precocious little boy, fond of big words, told me, at age three, he was "forostated" because he could not get something done. Gifted with a vivid imagination, John Paul would get a group of us to play out characters he was concocting as we performed. He would assign us very specific roles and correct us if he thought our performance was not compelling enough for his director's eye.

John Paul, age 3, at his home in Maryland

Smart, sweet, and easy-going, John Paul has always had the gift of gab. As he was growing up, we felt becoming a lawyer was in the cards, as he could, or tried, to persuade adults around him of whatever ideas he had at the time. Even as a young kid, he was also able to play intricate video games. He would patiently waste his time explaining the rules to me, since it was a given John Paul would beat everyone anyway. I remember his little sister walking out of the room mumbling in protest, "I am tired of getting killed."

His sister Katherine, known as Kat, is a straight A freshman college student. From an early age, she has shown her penchant and determination for self-dependence. When she was about eighteen months old, she made us wait until she finished tying her shoes in the middle of a restaurant floor. She would not accept help, so instead of making a scene, we patiently waited until she was satisfied with her job. At eighteen, she has decided to pursue a degree in child psychology.

Kat in 2008

A talented musician, she was a member of her high school's marching band as a sax player and performed in many public venues. She loves sports and politics, but her most defining trait is her love of learning. She follows her grades with a hawkish interest. When she is looking at her phone, it may not be a social call but her effort to find out what she made on a test or what her average grades are. No need to worry. They are all As. While shy and reserved around adults, Kat is the life of the party with her young friends. She maintains a busy life with books and friends as its foundation.

Julianne is Kat's contemporary and equally brilliant and talented. I am also proud of this eighteen-year-old who, most of the time, shows the maturity of an adult. She can still play and dream like a child, while performing the duties of a responsible daughter and older sister. Next to the front door, she has a long list of "to-do" reminders for her younger siblings, starting with "pick up your room and make your bed."

A seasoned ballet dancer, Julianne started her training at age four. I was in attendance at her first performance, sitting next to her other grandmother, Mary. Needless to say, both grandmoms were quite excited to watch the debut of our little ballerina. We were delighted to see the wonderful potential, as well as her extraordinary talent to follow instructions. We were laughing at seeing Julianne obsessed with standing where she was supposed to. She would look down at the marks on the floor and push away any other ballerina who would stand on her spot. We were proud, as we knew how hard this little girl had worked for her first public performance.

Julianne, the dancer, in 2017

My favorite part of the Christmas celebrations in the past was to fly to Dallas and watch that year's production of *The Nutcracker*. Julianne's roles advanced from snowflake to broom rat to fairy and to one of the dancers in "Waltz of the Flowers". Most roles were *en pointe*, and all were a testament to her determination and hard work. Every time, I was moved to tears, as beyond the graceful movements and complicated routines, I saw the intensity of her commitment to be her best.

Julianne continued her dedication to ballet for twelve years. Then she finally decided that her plans to become a physician like her great-grandfather would require all her focus and energy. She is enrolled as a freshman neuroscience student at the University of Texas at Dallas. I have always admired her ability to go after a dream, no matter how much work and effort it takes to make it happen.

Peter is also very special. Named after his late uncle, he shows an inclination toward scientific thinking. Just like his uncle, he has a twinkle in his eye and the most charming smile always at the ready. Serious and introspective, he is challenged by how things work. From an early age, he has shown a fascination for "putting things together." I would bring him presents with thousands of pieces, and before I could sit down for a family chat, Peter had already assembled it. He would find shortcuts, and modify the directions, which he would often find lacking. When you see Peter in his room talking, he is not talking to himself but to his best buddy at a distance. They are working out a computer issue or playing an elaborate video game.

When Peter was in the second grade, his mom would see on his report card yellow smiley faces next to "Discipline." It was not until the end of the school year that she found out the smiling faces had been yellow dots the teacher had used to indicate a warning. The "smiley" was entirely Peter's doing! Although technology is one of his passions, he also enjoys sports, such as fencing, baseball, and running, and his future plans include becoming a scientist.

Peter in a pensive moment in 2012

My namesake Andrea is the third of Julie and E.J.'s four children. Her name has been around for several generations, including her great-great-grandmother, her great-aunt, and her grandmother, and she is proud of being the next Andrea. She is always tickled when someone calls our name during my visits, and we both answer. She is her father's sidekick. Both avid fisher-people, Andrea is first up, and ready for their weekend adventure at the lake. She has inherited my strong character and is very definite about her choices.

Andrea, one of a kind, in 2009

Andrea has loved drawing and painting from an early age, when she would use any opportunity, including walls, paper napkins, and paper plates, to translate onto paper what her creative mind was seeing. As the artist she is, Andrea loves wild color combinations, which are evident in her dressing style. Loving boots, hats, and colors, she emerges from her dressing room as one of a kind.

She took ballet for a few years and also showed promise but was considering another choice. "Nani, should I be a dancer or an artist?"

My answer was, "Why not both? You should do what makes you the happiest."

She decided to work on her artistic inclinations, but as of late, she has had a change of heart and has begun ice-skating. I have enjoyed watching Andrea gracefully compete and win a number of awards in her current interest.

It also is moving to see a child of twelve searching for a future career with so much passion. On a recent road trip, she discussed several possibilities to consider—K9 police officer; work in a hospital; work at

Amy's ice cream shop; and, of course, professional ice skater. Perhaps soon, "painter" will be added back onto her list.

Young Max is an athlete, adept at anything technological, and loves to entertain. As a baby, he made us laugh by making faces and noises and, now that he is ten, by displaying his dada's adult sense of humor. When he was about four, while sitting next to me in a restaurant booth, he fell. Luckily the only injury was to his pride. For some reason, Max blamed me for the fall and spent most of the dinner showing his displeasure. We got in the car, and I heard a sweet voice from the backseat saying, "Nani, I know you didn't push me." And three seconds later, "May I play with your iPad?"

From an early age, Max has shown his athletic prowess. You could always find him atop a table precariously balanced, probably planning his next mischief. Learning to ride a bike was not an issue. Max just got on it and rode off, and when he needed to stop, he aimed at the grass. He did not need a trash can to help him stop, as his dad used to do at a similar age. As a Little League baseball player, Max is showing great promise as a catcher, a position held by his great-grandfather, grandfather, and dad.

Max and his kitten, 2013

Max is not only smart and funny, he is also very sweet. He has been texting me since he could only type symbols and emoticons, and now he has upgraded his communication skills by "FaceTiming." He has not indicated what he would like to be in the future, but for him, the sky is the limit.

So the six, the intellectual, the psychologist, the physician, the scientist, the artist, and the entertainer, are the lights of my life. They are blessings that compensate for the difficult times. Watching my grandchildren become who they aspire to be in their lives, supporting their efforts, and encouraging their search for what gives them joy are great sources of fulfillment for me as a grandparent. Seeing them respond to others with kindness and generosity makes me feel my time on this earth was well spent.

My Extended Family of Friends

A significant force in my support system is my family of friends. I define friendship as a link to aspects of the self that would never be revealed if friends were not there. Life is a much easier road to travel if in good company. If we are alone, we see ourselves as a flat reflection on a mirror. All we see are flaws.

The opposite is true when we reflect our image on a friend—and see virtues and possibilities as well. Good friends do not lie; they help me conjure a true image of who I am, an essential perspective to becoming whole and moving forward in life. In contrast, a simple image on a mirror could limit my possibilities by only reflecting what I see, curbing my growth as a person.

Like my parents, I love to be in the company of friends. The difference is they had an auditorium full, and I can fit mine in a closet, no pun intended. Our family of friends is best known as our "six-pack." There is nothing any of these six will not do for us.

One of them is also from Cuba, but we met in Madrid, New Mexico, at the home of friends, Senator Liz Stefanics and her partner, Linda Siegle. On our first acquaintance, I asked her if she knew a Cuban friend of mine, whose last name was the same as hers. How incredibly coincidental that my friend, whom I had not seen in several decades, happened to be her favorite aunt!

I had lived three houses from her paternal grandmother in the Sierra neighborhood of Havana, so I remember her handsome dad as a young medical student. Coincidences continue, since we agree that, very possibly, my father, who was a lung specialist, had cured her mother's tuberculosis back in Cuba.

My friends are the best people you could ever meet—funny, smart, generous, and always ready to help. Each plays a special role in our lives, and we value the strong bonds we have created.

Generally, bonds among friends are strong because we have chosen each other. Sometimes, these bonds are also possible with family members. And when that happens, it is generally a result of acceptance and respect for one another. I have developed a wonderful relationship with my second cousins, especially my Aunt Julita's handsome grandson, Lloyd, better known to us as "The Prince."

With Dutch roots, you would be misled if you thought of him as a super-Anglo. The fact is that despite his blond, blue-eyed looks, he sounds more Cuban when he speaks Spanish than I do. His focal point in life is world peace, and he presides over an organization that concentrates on training individuals from a young age to develop the skill of conflict resolution.

A well-traveled intellectual, Lloyd never misses the opportunity for new adventures. He recently returned from a business trip to eastern Africa, in which he combined work with enjoyment of safaris and visits to the amazing cloud forest. Two months later, he was off to Iceland, Mexico, and South America. His love of family is responsible for my reconnection with my blood relatives. A recent family reunion in Vermont, which I now plan to join every fall, was a happy reconnection with long lost cousins, who have now become an integral part of my support system.

Family reunion in Vermont, 2017
From left to right: Gastón and Eileen de los Reyes, Graciela de los Reyes Colón, Sari de los Reyes Devine, Beatriz de los Reyes Arsuaga, Lloyd Van Bylevelt
Second row: Ricardo (Ricky) Diez, me, and Ana Saavedra

Memories and messages my departed friends have left for me are also an integral part of my support system. Lynn, Elsa, Carmen and Penny left us too early, but their presence in my heart remains a constant inspiration.

Born in East Texas, Sarah Lynn McCollum (Lynn) moved to Santa Fe, New Mexico, in the late seventies. I met Lynn for the first time in 1981, on my initial visit to Santa Fe. I instantly realized that she was an old soul, full of wisdom and wit. The youngest daughter of Buster and Charleen, she had inherited their goodness and sense of fairness. This was a family that believed all of humankind deserved love and respect and acted accordingly.

Lynn also inherited the McCollum's musical gene. On a trip to San Francisco, Lynn; her sister, Ann; and a friend delighted me with their lovely harmony. I still see her sitting at her grand piano, playing by ear almost anything of your choice by only giving her a few notes as incentive. She also played the guitar and provided some fun entertainment in front of her lighted kiva on enchanting Santa Fe evenings. Those moments were magic, and so are the memories of the McCollum family friendship.

Unfortunately, Lynn also inherited her fervor to smoke. In 1991, she called with the good news that she had finally quit. "If scientists ever find out that cigarettes do not cause cancer, I am going to be pissed." It was only a few months later that we received a dreaded call that she had been hospitalized with a suspected stroke. We immediately flew to Santa Fe but not in time to say goodbye. She died on October 4 from brain cancer.

Her memorial felt as if she were there with us. On a stunning fall afternoon, in an outdoor ceremony surrounded by the beauty of music, friends, and the mountains that she had loved so much, we celebrated her presence in our lives. Lynn McCollum will always be remembered for her kindness, her wit, and her fun-loving personality. She took life seriously and learned to accept whatever came her way with her usual comment, "Life does not happen conveniently." Her mantra was a testament to her generous spirit: "I want to make those who come into contact with me feel better about themselves."

My Argentinean friend Elsa Zambosco was a trusted colleague and sidekick at the University of St. Thomas in Houston. We soon discovered we had a lot in common, beyond our chosen professions. We both had three children; our husbands were university professors; and we had married on the same day and year, at a church by the same name, in countries half the world apart. We were also young and enjoyed having a good time.

Elsa was a consummate theatre performer with a beautiful soprano voice. I was not much of an actor, and carrying a tune was not my forte. At Rice University, we both took part in a medieval play that took place in a convent. She was Mother Superior, and I was cast as a humble nun. After reciting my four lines, I stood behind Elsa along with the rest of the nunnery. When it came time for the song, she turned dramatically toward us, saying, *"Cantemos, hermanas"* (Let's sing, sisters). What the audience did not see was that Mother Superior was shushing me with her index finger. Needless to say, I had to fight hysterics to continue in my modest but serious role. There were so many unforgettable moments like this with my friend Elsa.

Our destinies took a different path when I finished my doctorate and was invited to join the University of Houston-Clear Lake. For many years, we did not see one another, until I heard she was suffering from leukemia, and I contacted her. We were both so happy to reconnect. It felt like no time had passed between us, and we laughed as heartily as when we were younger.

We visited a few times by phone, and Elsa promised to come to Santa Fe as soon as she was in remission. One night, I had a dream. I was hugging my friend and crying inconsolably. It was so real that I had to call her the next morning. Her daughter Vanessa shared the mournful news. My friend had left us the night before. She had kept her promise by visiting me in my dreams to bid her last farewell.

Carmen López was also born in Cuba. Her father had been a well-known urologist and a friend of my father's, but Carmen and I never met until we were both living in Houston, Texas. She was generous, loyal, and incredibly funny. She taught Spanish to my two boys at St. Thomas High School. My son E.J. always recounts how he had told his buddies, "Take Mrs. López in Spanish. She is a very nice friend of my mom's." He could not believe the transformation, once in class, where Carmen became a tough drill sergeant. His buddies never forgave him!

Her mother, also named Carmen, was a delicate and aristocratic woman, who oftentimes expressed shock at her daughter's choice of vocabulary, young Carmen's original versions of "four-letter words." Mama Carmen loved going places. It did not matter where to; she was always ready. My friend Carmen used to tell her, "Mother, I think you were a dog in another life. You hear keys and run to the door, purse in hand." Sadly, I lost my friend in 1990 after a two-year bout with lymphoma.

Following a long and hard-fought battle with colon cancer, we also lost Penny Kielpinski in February 2015. In her youth, she had been a champion gymnast. She maintained her love of competition and fearlessness for the rest of her life. There was nothing Penny would not try, regardless of the dangers involved. Her friend María recalls helplessly watching Penny with her broken leg on a ladder pursuing a chore that she would not postpone.

In her youth, she had also directed a choir, as well as played a variety of musical instruments. As an adult, she took up marimba, and became enough of an expert to delight us with several public performances. Penny also kept an extended bucket list that included African safaris, Grand Canyon adventures, and travels through Europe. She religiously checked her list to ensure absolute completion.

In the summer before Penny's death, Deb and I joined her and María on a memorable cruise of the Western Mediterranean. Penny was always first in line for adventure. Armed with her bucket list, she did not miss any opportunity for fun and excitement. Our last stop was Barcelona, where Penny had made arrangements to stay on the seventh floor of a quaint bed-and-breakfast. Since the elevator failed at times, I can still see her running up the stairs, without a sign of physical effort. In retrospect, I think of Penny as my inspiration to take pleasure in the moment and the courage to live with quality and joy until your time comes.

Penny, enjoying her marimba performance in 2014

My pets have also left inspiring memories. My Boston terriers, Missy and Prissy; the doxies that followed, Honey B, Annie, and Libby; and our cat, DOC (Damned Orange Cat) were loyal companions and masters of mischief. Their loyalty had no bounds, and there were so many lessons we learned from them. The "divine Miss L" (aka Libby), for instance, taught us how to keep our dignity even when fighting an undignified illness. To the end of her days, she expressed joy and appreciation for her place in our hearts.

Peter with Prissy in Houston, 1978

Recently, we lost our beloved seventeen-year-old Charlie, a long-haired, black-and-tan beauty. Charlie had let us know that being blind and deaf in her old age was not a reason for pity. After all, she knew her way to the backyard and to the pantry and, most definitely, to our hearts! Her death left a vacuum, but we are comforted by seeing her image in the clouds enjoying her new life in doggy heaven.

Memories of the love and loyalty of our departed furry friends are definitely an integral part of my support systems. As Deb always reminds me, "As long as you think of those who have passed on or mention them in conversation, they are still with us."

Now we are loved and entertained by our two other rambunctious dachshunds, Miss Lily and Abby, both with a penchant for squeaky toys. From these two, we have learned that their important place in our family is something they deserve, since both supply us with plenty of humor in our daily lives.

Spirituality and/or Religion?

In an effort to ensure that I am not missing out on something or doing too much of something else, I like to inventory what is going on in my life every once in a while. So it was one of those times that I realized that there was one important piece missing from my life puzzle—a religious community. For many years, I embraced the dichotomy of religion and spirituality as if they were mutually exclusive.

My last experience in the Catholic Church had been discouraging to say the least. I felt excluded as the young priest invited "only Catholics who had been to confession in the last two weeks" to partake in the sacrament. Although I felt I had confessed to God, I had forgotten that I needed an intermediary to be forgiven. I had been sacked. I became even more trapped in my belief that I was spiritual, so I felt that I did not need a place of worship. It was within me.

I had not realized how important "belonging" was. I was missing out on being a part of a community that shared my desire to be better and that supported each other in every step of our journeys. An Episcopal memorial service for my friend Penny brought me back to Church. I could not resist the feeling of being in the right place at the right time when the priest, Reverend Catherine Volland, turned to the congregation and warmly invited "all present to the table." Of course, I did, and so did everyone in the sacred home. Could it be possible that I had found the missing piece? I realized in time that I had deceived myself thinking I did not need to believe. I had just become aware that religion meant community. And what better base to share my gratitude for enjoying the good life?

Support systems are linked to the individual's survival, as they don't aim at changing the person but at proffering feedback and acceptance. My friend Lynn used to say, "If you see me looking weird, please tell me." To me, the litmus test for support systems is that they validate, not judge. I cannot fathom becoming an island within myself, without inviting others to share my joys and heartaches. Living in harmony with the environment, friends, family, and pets is how I feel the most delight and encouragement. My support system has always sustained me, and in my interactions, I have gained strength, knowledge, and enhanced appreciation of the moment.

CHAPTER 12

DEVELOPING INTERESTS AND DISTRACTIONS

I am a strong believer in seeking interests and distractions to counter-balance life's trials. They serve as our anchors to provide the stability and balance required to function successfully in our daily lives. Since needs, likes, dislikes, and interests vary from person to person, the "one size does not fit all" forces individuals to search for interests and distractions that best match their needs and aspirations. Beyond improving our overall attitude, these stress relievers will lengthen our lives and provide opportunities for pleasure and fun.

When my oldest son left for college, I realized my parenting duties were coming to an end. My three children were close in age, so I knew that, very soon, I would be an "empty nester." With my motherly responsibility diminished, I suddenly became aware that I did not know what to do with myself. My identity as a mother had to be replaced with a broader designation, but so many unanswered questions were paralyzing. I had been so absorbed in my children's lives that I really did not have enough self-knowledge to pursue interests of my own. A breakdown took me to a deep darkness, and I had no other choice than to be reborn emotionally.

In Search of Interests and Distractions

I realized that I had to regain control over my life and felt that developing interests and distractions was the best game plan. I proceeded to search for activities and projects I would enjoy. My goal was to discover an activity that would be pleasurable, while providing an opportunity to learn and grow. I tried the opera, theater, movies, concerts, and books—to no avail. I still had a sense of emptiness in my life. I even tried sports and, surprisingly, found an activity that gave me joy.

I joined a tennis camp, a tennis team, and my attitude about everything seemed to become sunnier. Enjoying the new activity helped me remove the hopelessness I had felt. Tennis became my hobby. I was a new person! I met new friends, became physically and emotionally healthier, and had a great time. The nuances I learned as a player gifted me with a lifelong interest in watching and enjoying professional tennis, baseball, football, and other sports. As medical findings have shown, interests and distractions decrease the risk of dementia and depression, ensuring a longer and healthier journey.

Both my parents were the embodiment of sanity, and I watched them through the years finding a respite from reality through their respective hobbies. Mother collected stamps and enjoyed learning about the various countries' history and politics, and she would insert in her albums information she had researched. When she passed away, she left her collection to me. It has provided me with hours of pleasure and discovery, often running into Mother's notes, which give me the feeling that Mother is with me.

We know that my father's love of trains came from childhood memories of his hometown in Cuba. As I watched him deal with the complexities of his life, I was trying to uncover the secret of how he kept his sense of humor and optimism intact. Here was a man who had lived through it all, and by his choice of profession, he also lived close to the misery of others. Yet, I always remember him sitting at the head of the table, entertaining all of us with his amusing stories. I am sure there was a part of him no one ever reached, but he always showed a man in control.

His trains were not only his hobby. They were a reaffirmation that he was keeping the child in him alive. I am convinced that his ability to protect the kid within gave him the emotional stability to surpass his hundredth birthday. He had an extensive collection of cars and locomotives, which he ran through cities and towns he had built from scratch.

I remember his scenic creations, little towns bustling with life—theatres showing the latest, *Casablanca*; post offices, stores, homes, schools, and children; and life recreated. A policeman was dutifully directing traffic, as there was no crime in these streets. His trains infused these towns with sparkle and animation. It was a tribute to life, a nirvana, where he was playing the Maker. What therapeutic exercise it must have been for this man who was the picture of sanity and well-being!

Cake granddaughter-in-law Barbara Barroso baked for Father's 100th birthday

His interests were many and varied, as he always kept his brilliant mind occupied and out of trouble. Studying the military history of the world, as well as keeping up with his vast knowledge of medicine, were integral parts of my father's daily routines. His intellectual pursuits competed with his love of baseball. Back home in Cuba, he owned an amateur team, the Pirates, playing some weekends as their catcher.

Dressed in their black-and-white uniforms, these players were doctors, cooks, and electricians who shared a common love of baseball, the national sport of Cuba. Together, they entertained a small audience, mostly family cheering in support. A business venture, it was not. It was an interest he pursued to balance his hectic existence.

Using Interests and Distractions as a Survival Tool

When my dad passed away in 2001, I was desperate to find solace. I also needed to search for a means to connect with his memory. Upon my return from his funeral, I saw a beautiful long-haired, black-and-tan dachshund at a pet store. It was love at first sight, but I decided to go home and give the puppy some thought. The more her image entered my thoughts, the more in love I became with this tiny creature.

Bright and early the next morning, I was at the store inquiring about her, since she was no longer in the window. An employee explained that the puppy was not well and was going to be returned to the breeders. The news made me sad, and I insisted on knowing what her problem was.

"Anemia," the salesman said.

"Oh, please, let us have her. We know she can recover with good treatment."

After promises that we would not return her (as if that were possible), we left for home with the adorable puppy, Charlie, named after my dad and after my late friend Charleen McCollum.

In a month, her anemia was gone, and she was delighting us with her high-spirited but sweet personality. Charlie, who lived a very long life, was born on my birthday and, through the years, gifted me with so much joy and comfort. Despite being blind and deaf, she was a happy senior, who could find her way around and enjoyed to the end her favorite pastimes, eating and cuddling.

Charlie at home in Houston in 2001

To enhance my spiritual bond with my dad, I also built a miniature train with a rural landscape equipped with homes, schools, shops, and a small church. An A-frame on a picturesque lake completed the scenery. My creation provided hours of enjoyment, always reliving the pleasure this hobby gave my dad through the years. Playing with my small train made me feel connected to him. I almost felt he was guiding me as I made the train bring life to the little town, just as he had done almost on a daily basis. Finding spiritual connections with those we miss in this life brings them back long enough to establish a new way to relate.

The "Wannabe" Architect Reemerges

A fellow university professor, Dr. Susanna Garrison, introduced me to the pleasures of building miniature dollhouses. I decided that the hobby promised therapeutic potential, as well as fun, so I purchased materials for a six-square-foot colonial house. I know I could have pursued a simpler project, but I have never been known for choosing the easiest route. Never having been too handy with tools, I was relying on Susie's experience.

After a few months, my yellow and green masterpiece was completed, with added electricity and furnishings. The dining room had a beautiful functioning crystal chandelier that added reality and warmth. A miniature oil painting of my grandmother, Mamaquico, hung above the piano in the living room, making the house feel like a long-lost home. The boys' room had to have a train, which I painstakingly constructed from the ground up. The yard was equipped with a swing set, a swimming pool, and a pet house for the two doxies that lived in the villa.

The project proved restorative, as my creation was replacing memories of homes lost in Cuba. Many dollhouses later, including one for granddaughter Andrea, I built my dream balsa wood gallery, *El Fénix*. The various wings showcase my paintings, photos, and sculptures on a tiny scale. Running out of space for this incredible hobby, I have become a generous dollhouse donor for children in the family.

Granddaughter Andrea's replica of her 2012 house

Compiling Bucket Lists

Dreaming and planning are very effective tools to combat an aging frame of mind, that is, thinking in habitual ways and seeing the world from a stagnant point of view. Once we stop exploring new experiences or interests, we have formally embraced old age. Remembering my friend Penny's last few years, I can't help but be persuaded that bucket lists are sources of hope. Not only is their presence a motivating tool, they also serve as reminders that there can be joy and promise, even at the end of the journey.

Penny's bucket list was extensive, and it was more of a checklist that she dutifully consulted. Penny dreamed big, but she was a good planner. So I am sure she satisfied most of her interests. At sixty-seven, already diagnosed with stage IV colon cancer, she joined a group on a camping trip to the Grand Canyon. She rafted down the Colorado River relishing the adventure, and loving her closeness to nature. Penny was inspired by the sights and sounds of her surroundings and by laughter and fun. She came back renewed with a new sense of future.

There was to be more travel on Penny's bucket list. The next year, she went on an African safari. She rode camels and ostriches, danced to new tunes, and played the marimba to the delight of other travelers. Europe followed, and a cruise to the Western Mediterranean in the summer of

2014 was her last. Her enjoyment of every experience during this trip was palpable and contagious; her energy and love of the moment, ever present. When she passed away in February 2015, she had done it all. Her bucket list complete, she was ready for her transition to the life of the spirit.

Like my friend Penny, I feel I have done a lot in my life. I have raised three children, received an education, worked since I was nineteen, made wonderful friends, traveled through most of the continents, and appreciated a variety of interests. I have enjoyed playing tennis and golf, skiing, horseback riding, and pursuing creative venues such as building dollhouses, writing, painting, and photography. But now, in my late seventies, as I reflect on Penny's inspiring example, I feel there is still so much more ahead to experience. Updating my bucket list has become my new calendar, and I hope that I become as devoted to it as Penny was to hers.

One of the things I want to seriously pursue is my writing. I did not realize how cathartic the writing experience can be. I took to writing about issues that bothered me with the intent of understanding how I could resolve them. I had even titled my effort *Book of Life I.* It was my best sleeping pill, when unsettling thoughts or issues would keep me awake at night. I had never considered myself a writer, until I realized that writing had been a thread throughout my life. I also feel that every person has at least one book to write, as every life is a remarkable set of short stories that can help inspire others to further the course of their journey.

Writing is also a great means of creating community, as, in order to have a writer, there have to be readers. A symbiotic relationship is created, and it continues forever to nurture those involved. I am intent on recording everything about my life, my family, my friends, and the tools I have used to make my journey more pleasant. I cannot think of a better therapy, a better mode to trade ideas, or a more pleasant way to learn from others in exchange for what I have learned.

Recently, I have joined a group of writers in a workshop led by a well-known artist, writer, and curator. We meet regularly for two hours to further develop our writing and thinking skills. Fellow writers are inspiring and generous in sharing ideas and experiences. Not only is writing pleasurable, it has also provided me with an opportunity for growth. I find this interest to be almost medicinal, as sometimes, worries and concerns are either resolved or seem much less menacing after seeing them translated to paper.

Creativity, in general, is a good line of attack in combating aging. In my view, there are two types of artists—those who have the talent to create and those who have the gift to recognize and celebrate beauty. Appreciating painters led me to painting as a tool to discover other aspects of my own being. That gift had escaped me during my early years. Fortunately, it was just dormant, so I was able to rely on it for many pleasurable hours later in my life. Thirteen years ago, I started painting. Although aware that my talent is not to be earthshaking, my artwork has developed immense appreciation for other artists and their art.

As a painter, I have dabbled in pastels, watercolor, and acrylic, but not in oils, since they require a degree of patience I do not have. I always say that, when God was doling out patience, I forgot to stand in line! I hope to transition from imitating talented artists to creating my own personal brand.

Perhaps another entry on my bucket list was inspired by a recent TV ad in which a guy tells his wife that he wants to continue being a bad golfer as long as he can. His words have motivated me to pursue this elusive sport again. Hundreds of hours of lessons seem to escape me, and that small ball dares me every time I try to confront it. Still, I find pleasure in the surroundings and in the friends that share an interest in the challenge.

Travel as an Interest

Travel is an experience that provides not only entertainment but also perspective. How many times we return home with a greater appreciation of what we have or where we have chosen to live. It is also wonderful to experience how other people with different languages and backgrounds approach their individual journeys. We not only learn new things, but also learn new ways to do old things. We learn the beauty of living in community and sharing existence with so many diverse peoples.

Sometimes travel is challenging, especially if we visit countries whose language we do not command. With the right attitude, even the scariest moments can turn into fun, at least when they become a story to tell. A few years ago, I was invited to the City Polytechnic of Hong Kong to present a professional paper with my colleague Steve Harmon. My language skills included my native Spanish; English; and a smattering of Italian, French, and Portuguese. Aside from the Romance languages, nothing else was in my repertoire. Cantonese, an entirely different language, was alien to me. As a tonal system, unlike English or Spanish, it relies on tones, rather than sentences, to convey meaning.

In an effort to be polite, my friend Steve and I asked a taxi driver, "How do you thank in Cantonese?"

His answer was, "Tipme."

We totally missed the playful intent of the driver and proceeded to use the newfound expression at every opportunity thereon. It was not until a Chinese American colleague, barely able to contain her laughter, told us how foolish we had sounded asking natives everywhere for a tip that we obviously did not intend to ask for!

Besides travel being a well-rounded learning experience, it also provides the opportunity to plan a future. And as such, it is an instrument of hope. I am in total agreement with my friend Cindy, who, when asked what her favorite trip was, replied, "My next one." If we choose to travel with the expectation of repeating a fun adventure we have experienced in the past, we might be disappointed. If we, on the other hand, embrace it as a new event, it may maximize the opportunity for an enjoyable learning experience.

The search for interests and distractions is a never-ending adventure, as our tastes and needs change over time. Recently, my eighty-something-year-old brother has found pleasure in learning Italian and French. He dreams of a European journey, where he can put into practice his recent accomplishments. He is already living his dream by just planning for it.

CHAPTER 13

LIFE IS A STRING OF MOMENTS

M uch like in a necklace, life is a collection of memories strung together. Each bead represents a past, a present, and a future, in a continuous sequence, repeating itself until the end of our journeys. We are aware that the past is a memory, the present is real, and the future uncertain.

Despite that realization, we fail to see how the three are interconnected. Every moment is linked to a past and a future, but too much emphasis on *what was* or *what will be* takes away from living *what is*. When my five-year-old brother Rod, the family philosopher, said, "Today is the yesterday of tomorrow," he was alerting us to the fact that, if we are not mindful of the present, it will become a fleeting memory.

Living in the Present

From childhood, I had trouble concentrating on one thing, as my mind would tend to wander. By definition, because I was a victim of an undiagnosed attention deficit disorder, I have always had trouble focusing on the task at hand. I was distracted by the future. As a youngster, if I was reading, I was thinking of riding my bike, of going to the beach, of so many activities other than my book. The skill to pay attention could be learned, but it would take me into young adulthood to finally master. Multitasking was my gift, and living the moment was one of my challenges.

Elementary school was a blur to me, which inexplicably I overcame.

I was absent from my own life and mostly lived in my traveling mind. Things were to change in high school, as my parents enrolled me in a highly challenging prep school. I had to figure out how to survive, and learning to focus on the moment became my lifeline. I still remember my math teacher, Dr. Gladys Japón, asking me a question, while I was distracted by looking out the classroom window. In the distance, I heard, "I am talking to her, and she is ignoring me."

The classmates' laughter brought me back from my daydreaming, and the embarrassment I felt made me realize I needed to do something about my lack of concentration. With great effort, I began to fight any thoughts other than those related to what was in front of me. I managed to meet the challenge of my new school because I learned to reserve my world of fiction for times when fantasizing was not an obstacle to functioning in the moment.

The older I become, the more I appreciate being able to embrace the now. My partner Deb reminds me, "We have today. Tomorrow is neither promised nor guaranteed. Make the best of it." There have been so many times I have not followed her advice and I have missed present moments to make room for uncertainty. When all the planning goes out the window, because life happens differently from what I had envisioned, I know I did it again!

This Was One of Those Days

Everything was planned out. I woke up early, went for my walk, and got ready to attend my weekly writing group. I left with plenty of time, so I would not be late. The weekly meeting is led by Sara Eyestone, a well-known painter and writer who serves as La Posada de Santa Fe's art curator.

The trip to class was uneventful. Traffic was light, and the east sun managed not to disturb my driving. I was in a great mood, looking forward to a fun and productive writing session. As I got close to East Palace Avenue, I noticed flashing lights, a fire truck, and an ambulance—all ominous symbols of a serious accident. There was a lot of glass at the intersection and a couple of cars in sight, one of them totaled.

There was more I could not see from my vantage point. A fleeting thought that it could be one of my peers was quickly dismissed, and I turned right to continue to the hotel entrance. I was met by the valet, who informed me, "There is no class today," and, pointing to the corner, added "That was Sara."

Of course, in the midst of my shock, my first question was, "Is she okay?"

I was assured she would be, as she had been able to phone her sister, despite the fact that her head had hit the windshield.

I left the place in a very different mood than when I had just arrived. I didn't know much more than what I had been told—that Sara had been taken to the hospital in the company of her sister. There was nothing I could do but wait. I left for home, my thoughts taken over by the misfortune of the accident, concern about Sara, and worry for unknown others also involved.

Many other thoughts entered my mind. Had we as a group been thankful enough for her many talents and her generosity to share them with us? Had we taken for granted the wonderful sessions, in which, as participants, we were becoming better writers?

We know moments are fleeting. But unfortunately, we need reminders to bring us back to the present. Most of the time, we replace the enjoyment of the now, the appreciation for being a part of it, with the figment of a future that may never happen. I had enjoyed my morning walk, the freshness left by the night rain, the beautiful clouds embellishing the desert sky. Had I known what was to transpire, I would have felt more gratitude for being a part of that experience. I learned, again, that I need to take pleasure in savoring what is real and not rush through these moments to make room for a moment that might not be as gratifying.

Learning the Lesson

Today, I decided to concentrate on the pleasures of my morning walk. So instead of counting the minutes per mile, my heart rate, calories burned, and so forth, I focused on my environment. I stopped to admire a hummingbird moth industriously sipping the nectar of lavender blossoms. I noticed that there was an uncanny resemblance to the avian humming-bird, but it lacked the aura of its namesake.

The experience brought to mind how many lives around us we ignore as we go about our business—particularly, creatures sharing the same space, the same history, yet only intersecting ours by chance. I wonder about other humans who cross our paths seemingly unaware of our existence—parallel universes that continue to create complex life stories we may never get to hear.

In the background, the Sangre the Cristo mountains, dubbed "Sangres" by the locals

I also stopped to admire the distant view, the Jemez Mountains to my left and Sangre de Cristo to my right attesting to the life before me and beyond—silent, majestic, imposing forms of nature seemingly un-affected by my presence. I stopped to look at them, to admire the hand of the artist that created them.

In the distance looking west, I could see vehicles moving fast on I-25 connecting Santa Fe to Albuquerque. They resembled a busy ant colony. The scene reminded me of my dad's model train. The memory brought me a smile. I thought of the pleasure my father derived from playing God by creating towns and scenery that rivaled those we see around us. I smiled again. By the time I returned from my walk, I felt strengthened, not so much by the exercise, but by the power of happy memories, by the enjoyment of having been in the moment.

Living in the Future

When my three children were very little, I spent my days dreaming and planning for the day when I would complete my university studies and become a professional. I felt it was important to invest in my family's future but maybe I had put too much effort in improving something that was already fine. The family just needed me to be more of a participant in our everyday life.

I wish that I had taken the time to focus on each child—to memorize their mannerisms, their sense of humor, all the little things that made them special. It would have been enjoyable to know what they preferred for dinner and make a special effort to indulge each and every one of them. I failed to do that. I was in a hurry to improve their lives.

My days were consumed with dreams of a better life. Lucky for us, the better life did come, but it came at a price. I was no longer young, and the children, now wonderful adults, had already left the nest to pursue life on their own. I wish this aspect of my life had taught me a lesson—enjoy the moment, capture the now, and live it with intensity.

However, that important lesson escaped me, and I continued my journey planning the future, trying to improve a present that only needed for me to recognize that I was a part of it. Having rushed through these moments of my life was one of my most burdensome regrets. Finally, I realized that the past was gone, and I could not fix my mistakes. I could only learn not to repeat their history.

When I was younger, I never thought that we would have to leave our homeland. In my mind, I was going to spend the rest of my days on my beautiful island surrounded by my family, and friends I had known from an early age. Evidently, that was not to be. My parents had diligently prepared us for a future that never happened. They taught us the values of our culture and passed on the tools to survive in that environment. The future we would face was radically different, making those survival tools lose their relevance.

Every time I get sick, I vow not to take my health for granted and to fully appreciate the feeling of wellness. Unfortunately, the promise does not last, and my focus, once again, turns to the future. I am trying to remember to celebrate each day when I can say, "I feel great today," to avoid going from one sickness event to another. Too much emphasis on what is due tomorrow or on future activities that do not relate to today diminish possibilities of appreciating the moment.

Calendars should not become the driving force of my life. Lists, dates, commitments, and appointments with the future take me away from the pleasures of the now. Being future-oriented, however, is not necessarily at odds with embracing the present moment (although we must recognize that the future generally happens but hardly ever the way we planned it). This reality suggests that I should not skip over the now, to exclusively place my attention on some uncertain prospect.

A friend, in response to my excitement about something that has not yet happened, always warns me, "I don't get excited until the moment arrives. I hate to be disappointed." I see a point in her words, but I would rather enjoy my excitement now, and deal with disappointment, when and if it were to happen. Perhaps, transporting a future event to the present is not as bad as ignoring the moment altogether. When we built our dream home, I had lots of pleasure planning, designing, selecting color schemes, researching plants, and shopping for special pieces. This is a different kind of looking at the future. By transplanting my project to the present, I was already savoring the excitement of what it could become. In a way, the future was not competing with the present but, rather, complementing it.

Balancing the Moment in a High-Tech Environment

It is not possible to live in the past, because circumstances have changed. It is likewise impossible to live in a future that constantly transforms itself into an entirely different environment, posing new challenges and rewards for those who dare adapt. This reality forces me to live in the moment, while keeping an eye on what I need to do to stay in touch with the changing world and not be left behind.

In my lifespan, I have witnessed a transformation from "low-tech"—rotary phones, no television, manual transmission vehicles with hand-cranked windows—to a world of advanced technology dominated by the internet. Staying abreast of the new tools to navigate and survive our environment is the greatest challenge to my mindful state. If I choose not to keep up with the times, then I have chosen to live in the past. On the surface, it seems contradictory that, to stay in the present, I have to think of the future. But this duality, enjoying the now while moving on, is called balance.

Adapting to the changes brought about by our new world is not easy, as society's value systems dramatically change to keep up with the technological advancements. As discussed in an earlier chapter, in my day, the elderly occupied a position of reverence, as the purveyors of wisdom. The young sought advice from the older generation, who, at their passing, would confer their role to the next generation. In the world of today, the preeminent relationship is reversed. The young have the knowledge, hence the power to advise and direct the older generation to successfully traverse the challenges of a technology-driven environment.

Granddaughter Andrea texting on her way to her First Holy Communion

I was fortunate that my professional life developed in a university setting, where retraining was a vital component of my ability to perform my duties. I became a computer aficionada and used every opportunity to become proficient in the new medium. I remember with awe the first time I used the mysterious internet. I was mesmerized but realized at the same time that the present moment had become more complex. The internet eventually became the sole medium for a transforming world, a world of smart phones, tablets, and social media. Keeping up with its swift pace came to be a necessary condition to living in the moment.

Creating Space for New Beginnings

Taking life a moment at a time paves the way to creating new beginnings. It was 1981, and I had just turned forty. For the first time in years, I actually felt young and hopeful. After replacing a professor on temporary leave the year before, I had been invited to join the University of Houston-Clear Lake faculty in a tenure-track position. My professional life was promising, being a part of a campus respected for its high academic standards.

My three children were doing well, and although my finances were challenging, we seemed to have a bright future ahead. I was mindful that things were going well, and I started taking better care of myself. I had stopped drinking in excess, lost weight, and probably looked my best. My hair was black and short, pixie style, and contact lenses completed the appearance. Life was good, and good attracts better! I had just met a wonderful person, one of my students, and to be truthful, I was smitten. When the course ended and I turned her grade in, I went straight to a phone and called for a date. Feelings were mutual, and we spent the next twenty-three years as partners, until our relationship took us in separate directions.

Our first trip together in summer 1981 was to Santa Fe, New Mexico, to meet her sister, Lynn, who had moved from Texas. I remember her warmth as she opened the door and, with a friendly squeeze, made me feel at ease. "Welcome! This is your home." Her words ring true to this day, and I still sense her sweet and generous demeanor.

From that moment on, we looked forward to our yearly visits, which became more frequent as time passed. Eventually, the past melded with the present, and Santa Fe became our home and our new beginning.

Taking Risks

Many people negate future happenings because of fear, others because they habitually say no to uncertainty. And to me, *no* is not an answer; it is an attitude. In both cases, these individuals have not allowed novelty to enter their lives. Risk taking is a necessary approach to the future, as it opens doors to more pleasurable experiences. Taking risks may also be an opportunity encountered, when attempting to live in the moment. If I say no to the future, I may be depriving myself of a more enjoyable present.

Risk taking can happen either intentionally or by coincidentally finding oneself in a certain place at a certain time. Whether individuals are intentional risk takers or accidental ones, their lives move from an instant past to an unexpected new and conceivably more exciting moment. Life without risk becomes stagnant, like wheels turning in place. If the moment suggests to me that I should leap into action, I do not allow fear to stop me. Fortunately for me, I have experienced and benefited from both forms of risk taking.

Early Encounter with Risk: Tía Loló's Escape

This event took place on a dark Havana night in 1959, just a few months after the Castro takeover of the island. My family was being persecuted because of its relationship to the previous government. My brother Carlos had married one of the nieces of Batista's prime minister, and Batista himself had acted as a witness to their wedding. Carlos' family-in-law had mostly left for exile, but an aunt, sweet Tía Loló, was still in hiding. Her only connection to Batista was her brother and a job as director of Maternidad Obrera, a hospital for low-income women.

Tía Loló had to move every few days, from one secret place to another, to stay out of danger. These escapades occurred at night to ensure her safety. Although I was not a licensed driver, in a lawless environment, that fact was a minor detail. By default, I became her conduit to a secure getaway.

When I arrived at Tía Loló's hideout, she was ready with her numerous pieces of luggage and dark glasses. With the sun long gone, I let her know this made her appear more suspicious. She followed my advice, and the three of us, Loló, her luggage, and I, embarked on a risky venture to procure another safe house in the middle of the night.

I drove carefully and slowly, much like people who had had one too many drinks and, with the angels on our side, managed a successful ride.

Days later, the family arranged for her departure to the United States, where Tia Loló lived a full life until her eighties. This time, living in the moment and taking the risk of reacting with determination allowed us to escape the life-and-death perils we had faced.

Embarking on New Adventures

One of my favorite life passages was learning to ski at age forty-five, which happened to also be the age when I finally had my life in order. Sadly, four years before, I had lost my son Peter. However, his constant presence in my life has always served as an inspiration to work on becoming a better person and to try doing things I have never done before. At the time, I had not discovered too many favorite interests or hobbies, as my life had only been about working, raising children as a single mother, and going to school. I realized that there was a connection between having interests, staying sane, and having an exciting life. The memory of my ever-present son was also motivating me to live, to learn new things, and to introduce adventure into my life.

Learning to snow ski at forty-five was quite the challenge, since my home base had been a tropical island, where sea, not mountains, and summer, not winter, were my year-round entertainment sources. Despite this fact, I found it exhilarating to ski down a slope covered in powder with the sounds of silence highlighted by snowflakes drumming my face. We planned western ski trips to Utah, Colorado, and New Mexico, enjoying what each state had to offer.

I loved the winter village of Park City, Utah, where I felt like I was part of a Christmas card, and the steep and stunning terrains of Colorado and New Mexico. So much beauty around us made me feel that, if that day were to be my last, I had seen the face of God.

On a professional trip to Wyoming, I planned to take a side ski trip to Snowy Range, thirty miles west of Laramie. At the time, it was a well-kept secret, since natives wanted to ensure tourists would not invade the area. I got in my rental car, equipment ready, no cell phone, no GPS, and no blankets—just a sense of adventure I had never felt before.

The road, its sides, everything in sight was draped in snow. For an islander, it was surprising to me that I was comfortable being the only car on the road under such blanketing conditions. Armed with a paper map, I made it to the ski basin at about midmorning. I only saw two other people—the lift operator and a bear of a bearded man—who, I assumed, was another crazy skier. I chose a beginner slope that gave me enough of a challenge, as very soon I was stuck in a narrow flat trail that led to a more challenging one. I succeeded in freeing myself after some struggling, and, thankfully, the rest of the descent was flawless.

Suddenly, I realized what I was doing with a tad of anxiety. I started thinking to myself, *What on earth are you doing here? Are you nuts? Get back in the car and go to a safer place.* All these warning messages discouraged me from continuing my adventure. I got back in my rental car and mapped my return, not without stopping first for a buffalo burger. Not usually attracted to meat, I found lunch absolutely extraordinary.

By two o'clock, I was back at the bed-and-breakfast, safe, revitalized by the adventure, and seeing myself in a new light, as an extreme sports adventurer! I did not know I had it in me to defy logic in such a way, but it felt gratifying to feel so fearless. In retrospect, I feel Peter, my guardian angel, was looking after me and, again with his disarming grin, was saying, "Mom, I am so proud of you."

One thing we know for sure is that life happens. We might as well make it adventurous and exciting and, most importantly, be there. "Life is a dance. Mindfulness is witnessing the dance" (Amit Ray, *Mindfulness: Living in the Moment – Living in the Breath*).

PART V

THE JOURNEY CONTINUES

CHAPTER 14

SURVIVING MAJOR LIFE TSUNAMIS

Sometimes life presents us with moments of real or perceived loss that severely threaten our well-being. In my case, those moments are evidenced in the death of loved ones, the loss of a homeland, and the end of significant relationships. Any of these events can take us to the depths of despair, a dark place with seemingly interminable hopelessness. Fortunately, the passing of time has a healing effect in restoring the light.

I consider having survived a number of bumps along the road my highest personal triumph. In many instances, those bumps have felt like indomitable mountains. But with good fortune on my side, I have successfully climbed to their summit. From there, I have seen infinity and its promises.

The Passing of Someone Loved

The most difficult heartache for a mother is the loss of a child. No words can describe the devastation it provokes. My son Peter was only twenty when a tragic mishap claimed his life and the lives of three of his teenage friends. Four mothers overwhelmingly grieved, even though the intense pain we felt was not sufficient to bring our children back. At the moment, there was nothing that could console us. Nor was there an indication that the sorrow would become bearable with time.

Peter in 1966

I wish I had known then that grief itself has restorative powers, in that it brought to light strength I did not know I possessed. Happier memories start the process of entertaining positive thoughts. Peter's life was not futile. It was an inspiration, the very motivation for me to persevere. I started thinking that he made his transition at a time when his life was still rosy. I imagined all the misery he might have experienced had he lived longer. I was sustained by his memories and by a spiritual bond that has never abandoned me. Many years later, I established a memorial scholarship in his name at the University of Houston-Clear Lake. Every semester, I am delighted to see how Peter's memory still helps many other youngsters in pursuing their dreams. I know that he continues to make a difference.

The passing of loved ones is definitely the most difficult climb; one's energy and determination to continue the journey are compromised. Working at staying sane during those challenging times has been my focus. Surrounding myself with family, friends, and interests has given me support to stay the course. Oftentimes, I was able to find humor, making it easier to face challenges head-on. My tendency to see the glass half-full has always been an advantage in my search for strength and meaning in life.

Death is itself a learning experience. We either accept the fact that it happens to everyone or refuse to think about it. I believe that death does not mark the end of the journey but rather its continuation, allowing us to experience the complete life cycle. Creatures of this world have been crafted with precision and purpose, a fact that indicates to me the existence of a higher level of destiny.

Exile: Making Lemonade out of Lemons

A different type of loss, but still highly distressing, was the loss of my homeland. When I left Cuba several decades ago, I suspected it was the point of no return. As newlyweds, my husband and I left to start our new life with sixty pounds of luggage, and a total of five dollars, in itself a challenging circumstance. I just pushed forward with the conviction that this tunnel would be short.

Facing Prejudice

Of all the negative experiences we face as immigrants, for me racism was the most difficult to survive; it assaults the very core of one's identity. I had not experienced that type of hatred before, since I came from a culture where my race and class represented the mainstream. A few weeks after moving to Miami, I was stricken with a very painful kidney stone. I was in dire need of finding a phone to seek help. Since we did not own one, I proceeded to the manager's apartment, seeing the sign "Manager on Duty" clearly displayed. I explained my predicament to a woman who seemed indifferent to my request for a phone. Without making eye contact, she brusquely responded, "There is a public phone outside," and simply closed her door in my face.

Doubled up in pain, I crossed the courtyard and went back to our apartment in search of change. A trip that should take under two minutes felt like an eternity. I found enough coins to call my aunt, who being her kind self, came to my rescue. I had to leave a note for my husband letting him know that I was being taken to Mercy Hospital in Coconut Grove.

Fortunately, it did not take long for him to appear in the emergency waiting room, where he found me in a wheelchair and my aunt holding my hand. Since we had no insurance, the hospital would not admit me unless we could deposit $200 cash. He left to obtain the required funds so I could be helped. He was back in an hour, and I was finally admitted. The saga had just begun.

I also did not realize then that the apartment manager's reaction was the result of her prejudice against the wave of Cubans that had recently arrived, and I was one of them. Something must have justified in her mind and heart her disregard for the dilemma of someone in need. At the time, I had to address my physical pain first. But after it was remedied, I started thinking about the events that had transpired. I could have folded and given into the negativity of the manager's message. Fortunately, something stronger within me took over and, in its place, made me feel sorry for the woman. I did not understand how anyone could so cruelly ignore someone else's obvious pain and allow her hatred to overcome her compassion.

As years have passed, this incident has confirmed that "what" or "who" I am does not have to be determined by the opinion of others but by the trust and confidence I have in myself. Whatever happened to the manager, I hope she was able to develop an appreciation for all human life. If her anger and hatred toward others continued to manifest throughout her life, I assume she lived a miserable existence.

In retrospect, I had experienced prejudice for the first time. I realized I was a minority both as a Cuban and, worse, a poor Cuban. I also thought of the irony in the hospital's name. What was so merciful in what they had put me through? The passage of time has relieved the anger and hurt I felt at the time.

I have wondered what these experiences could have caused to my self-esteem had I lived in that kind of environment all my life. I learned the hard way that making decisions against someone based on hate and ignorance leads nowhere. Prejudice blinds the hater and hurts the innocent, who did not choose race, status, or birthplace. "Do you know what we call opinion in the absence of evidence? We call it prejudice" (Michael Crichton, *State of Fear*).

Tackling Cultural Adaptation

To adapt to life in the United States, the hardest lesson for me was to figure out its cultural standards so that I could start feeling at home in the unfamiliar surroundings. I went through countless humorous, as well as painful, experiences in trying to acclimate to life in my adopted motherland. I spoke English well but still had a lot to learn about the country's value system, which after all determines one's future position and opportunities.

Living as an observer of the country's daily events is the greatest drawback in trying to belong and participate in a new culture. I have made every effort to adapt to life among people different from me, by respecting their established rules and mores and by trying to understand their ways of thinking and behaving. This approach has assured me a place at the table. If you never become part of your adopted society, there is little opportunity from its fringes to make a difference in your life or in the lives of others.

Experience had already told me that friendship in my new world was a support system, not the melding of close friends into one being, as it had been for me before. I learned the value of the self and the need to respect others' choices, desires, and aspirations. As part of my adaptation efforts, I also recognized the importance of being a distinct individual who does not need group validation but who relies on personal satisfaction about my decisions and their impending outcomes. I became in charge of being, and becoming, the person I wanted to be.

Although our family choice for a new home was the United States, the American dream was neither easy to attain nor even possible for some. In following its path, there were many challenges and disappointments and no guaranteed results. We had to be open to learning new things, taking risks, and respecting the value system of the new environment. Learning what was adequate or practical and seeking to replace behaviors that clashed facilitated a less painful crossover. Education has been a key in reaching the dream, and I am grateful to have had the courage to pursue the opportunities that have come my way.

Anti-Immigrant Mood Sweeping the United States

Most immigrants have suffered the distress of leaving their familiar environments and seeking sanctuary elsewhere. Those who have not been through this type of experience may underestimate what is at stake. So many times, I have been affronted by self-proclaimed intellectuals, who, after spending a few days in Cuba, return with enthusiastic comments about the advantages of the Castro regime. These individuals do not realize that it is less traumatic to observe history than to live it. The grief caused by the loss of a homeland is almost inexplicable for those who have never left their democratic and sheltered environment.

As of late, anti-immigrant sentiments have monopolized the national discourse in the United States, making survival and adaptation even more problematic for those seeking refuge. In a country of immigrants, it is hard to understand how some people determine who belongs and who does not. Everyone deserves a place, since we all share the privilege of birth and death. The only factor partially under our control is how we interpret and carry out our journey. Success is not measured by our accomplishments alone but, rather, by how we feel about ourselves and the lifestyle we have chosen. If we are satisfied, we will very likely project a certain confidence to others, and that, in turn, promotes respect and acceptance.

End of a Friendship

Ending a friendship or a significant relationship can be construed as a calamity in the moment. We are always ready for a relationship's beginnings because they signal promise, but endings are hardly ever a welcome experience. Sometimes, we can foresee the end of the road, but wishful thinking keeps us hopeful. Since we consider an end a failure, we stubbornly fight to keep the vanishing relationship going.

In looking back, I realized how a breakup can often be everyone's solution. Relationship expert Staci Welch-Bartley has persuaded me, "When things seem to fall apart, know that they are actually falling into place." Learning this lesson early on would have spared much heartache, even if the setting were a divorce, where children were involved. As I once told my parents, "My problem is a bad marriage. Ending it is the solution." This reality also applied to the ending of other relationships.

My childhood friendships survived only in memories; life took those friends and me in separate directions, and reconnections have been difficult. We have coped with life in diverse ways and have become different people. My few encounters with some of those friends have been disappointing. We agree on little and dream different dreams, a discouraging beginning on which to forge new relationships. I have decided that memories are more valuable to me than the ache of disillusionment.

To balance this loss, other friendships have emerged. Dr. Enrique Johanet, for one, has reappeared in our lives to provide support and encouragement. We lived around the corner from each other in Havana, but age differences kept us in separate spaces. As seniors, we are on a par now, and a beautiful friendship has developed. There is past history to connect us; he was my father's student in medical school and remembers him with great esteem. We are also connected by respect and admiration for what each of us has accomplished in life. Much like my friendship with Enrique, other special friendships have sustained me through thick and thin.

Other Life Trials

A challenge is an invitation to find an answer to what ails. Taking a step at a time with the conviction that each step is on solid ground, we gradually move toward a resolution. I find it essential to avoid giving into negativity by moving on with the confidence that there is a light at the end of the tunnel.

Hitting Bottom

I would compare my thirties to a volcano erupting. I had not realized I was a ticking bomb until a psychiatrist friend told me that my way of handling stress, keeping everything to myself, was not healthy. He happened to be correct.

My mother's death was a sobering moment after my divorce three years earlier. My life was spinning out of control, and a regretful relationship made matters worse. Mother had been my advocate and steadfast supporter. Now she was gone, and I had to face the music alone. My job was a dead end, which did little to sustain me. In addition, being a single mother of three teenagers failed to provide balance in my already complicated circumstances.

The fact that alcohol had become my escape du jour made my predicament even more challenging. One ray of sunshine had been my doctoral studies at the University of Houston. I started to see this project as the best way out of my grim existence. This would not come easily. I woke up one day to realize that my family's destiny was in my hands.

Something drastic needed to be done—and soon. I took myself to my friend Dr. Ozora F. Young and asked for help. She made a few phone calls, and the next day, I was a patient on the seventh floor of Herman Hospital in Houston, under suicide watch. Fortunately, very soon the doctors realized that I was there because I wanted to live and had sought professional help in sorting out how to best do it.

A few days later, I left the hospital with a solid resolve to face my challenges. I had discovered that sometimes you have to hit bottom to find hope and be reborn. I managed to get my doctoral degree, find a more stimulating job at the University of Houston-Clear Lake, and bid alcohol abuse farewell.

The ones that made a difference. E.J., Peter, and Flori in 1976

I was on the mend and ready for the rest of my journey. Today, I am at peace with myself. It helps that I love activity and pursue interests that channel my anxieties into more positive terrain. If anxiety shows its ugly face, I take to my writing, which invariably helps me locate its source so I can do something about it.

Disowned by the Roman Church

I have always believed that the mission of any church is to invite and serve those in need. My experience has unfortunately proven this belief mistaken. Rather than feeling welcome and supported, I have experienced rejection. As I said earlier, not too long ago, I attended a Catholic funeral Mass for the mother of a good friend. As they were preparing for communion, the young priest addressed the faithful with a warning. His message was direct and unyielding regarding who was invited to the table. By only allowing those from his Roman faith in good standing (recent confession), I felt that the priest was excluding the very ones who might have needed the sacrament the most. In my eyes, the church had neglected its mission to serve those who needed to be "saved" and become an exclusive agent for those who have been made to believe they don't need saving.

Although not a religionist, my deep spirituality connects me with the rest of creation. Belonging to my church connects me with others who pray. I am very grateful for my place in life and for the love that surrounds me. Being conscious of the gifts I have received, I am not only appreciative but also prayerful. I ask for courage and strength to continue my journey in good spirits. My prayers are addressed to my God, the preternatural force that can hear them. Perhaps those who have a greater gift of faith have an easier journey, but I am confident that I will not be sentenced to everlasting suffering for having the courage to be true to self.

Experiencing Dark Nights

Dark nights are vital facets of our journey. I truly believe that darkness exists so that we can embrace and appreciate the light that habitually follows. Learning to confront rather than disregard our personal darkness is a healthy step toward attaining peace of mind. Unfortunately, there are no pat answers to better tackle the experience than to face the root cause head-on.

Those of us who have lived through hurricanes know that the eye, or center, of the storm is the most tranquil. We can always find a peaceful center in life's struggles, where we can take refuge and prepare to confront whatever is to come. For me, the best antidote to the dark nights is to take time to write down what I feel at the moment. It leads me to understand reasons for my anxiety or worry, and from there, I start seeing issues with more clarity. What seemed insurmountable before becomes almost ready for a resolution.

Sometimes our dreams are unpleasant, almost frightening, and we wake up afraid to go back to sleep. Not too long ago, I was awakened at two in the morning by such a dream. In it, I was running away from an unknown source, almost flying through streets that reminded me of Rome. I arrived at a large plaza occupied by armed soldiers. We seemed to be under attack, but the soldiers assured us that we were safe. I was looking for a big boat that was supposed to take me home. I did not seem to be alone; I had the feeling I was talking to someone. We went through the lobby of an elegant hotel and finally arrived at a pier. There was no boat, only darkness. I decided to go back but woke up before reaching a destination. After waking up, I felt uneasy, unnerved for no apparent reason.

I wanted to know the meaning of my dream and restore my serenity. I wrote down the following words: "Darkness, a boat, soldiers, war, no return, go back to what I left." I continued my experiment, and this time I wrote sentences: "Darkness is the unknown, and we must not give into it." "The answer, the interpretation of a dream, is not necessarily the most obvious." I finally decided that the message in my dream was to always keep moving to a safe place, where I could think clearly.

I realized that the soldiers in my dream meant that I was being protected—that I was safe and not alone. I wrote two more sentences: "Don't be afraid. Have trust." It took me forty-five minutes to conquer my apprehension, and I was able to go back to a quiet sleep.

I believe that the difference between a nightmare and a dream is in how we use the experience. If a problematic dream is left unresolved, it becomes a nightmare. In deciding to write down what came to mind, I ended up extracting a positive message that restored my serenity.

Engaging in long walks also helps me find peace of mind, especially when I concentrate on the miracles of nature, a wildflower, a butterfly, a hummingbird. Rather than feed the dark thoughts, I replace them with beauty, with appreciation of what surrounds all of us. Since there is not a single answer that fits everyone in dealing with dark episodes, it is important that we find our own special technique to find the light. Some people meditate; others read, pray, or concentrate on an interest or creative endeavor.

Many times, people worry about vague, formless fears that, when narrowed down to a concrete thought, become less formidable and easier to resolve. Whatever suits the person in making the darkness concrete and manageable leads to a way out. Only then have we led ourselves to the light.

We must wage war against negativity and find acceptance when the cards dealt to us point to a losing game. A heavy heart is a part of life. How we deal with it is our choice. A quotation attributed to author and artist Vivian Greene eloquently affirms this: "Life isn't about waiting for the storm to pass. It's about learning to dance in the rain."

CHAPTER 15

TO AGE OR NOT TO AGE: LESSONS LEARNED

I am not trying to distort Shakespeare's famous words but, rather, borrow some of his wisdom to express my thoughts. If aging were a choice, I wonder how many takers there would be? If humans were wine, old cars, or old furniture, aging would be more appreciated. Nothing wrong with "aged to perfection," "a classic," or an "antique." But plain "old" is somewhat less appealing. Despite these attitudes about age, we must accept that growing old is a process that few escape, and those who do are no longer with us. The sooner we admit this certainty, the easier it will be to progress through our journey with less anxiety.

I was always in awe observing my father's aging process. Two things stood out—acceptance and attitude. In his 101 years of being, he seemed to accept life as it happened to him. Always looking for a rosier explanation of events, he once shared with me how he dealt with life in exile. In his own words, "I have been married twice. My first wife, Cuba, was gorgeous, and I loved her very much. She is no longer. I am fortunate to have married a second time, to the United States, who is equally beautiful but in a very different way. If I compare them, nobody wins. If I don't, I have the opportunity for happiness ever after. For this to happen, I cannot be *amarrado a la guayaba* (tied to the guava, a favorite Cuban fruit.)" He believed in his words.

Not a man who looked back and wished things were different, he moved on, embracing his lot in life. For my father, age was an attitude. He chose to overlook the aches and pains of aging and to concentrate on the positive attributes he gained, particularly character, wisdom, and self-confidence. He lived a difficult life, which included participating in war, losing loved ones, and losing his homeland. But none of these challenges diminished his optimism and sense of humor about his journey. When my daughter, Flori, turned thirty, she was not thrilled, so Dad tried to cheer her up: "Don't worry, *mi hijita*. I have been there three times."

Learning from Experience

There are so many lessons that we could learn from our mistakes. Unfortunately, sometimes those lessons fail to stick. One lesson I take to heart is learning to accept change as inevitable and as more of an opportunity than as a sign of potential trouble. In my experience, change occurs in two ways. We have "aha" moments, when we unexpectedly gain awareness of a reality. The signature of these moments is when we see clearly the reasons something is not working or when we are surprised to find a long-sought solution to a problem. Aha moments give us the opportunity to readily change in light of our sudden discovery.

Regrettably, not all learning from experience happens with such ease. Sometimes, the message is hidden, and we must go through the process of "hard learning" or grief to uncover its meaning. Not too long ago, I experienced a dreadful reaction to a medication, which rendered me unable to walk without excruciating pain. My wonderful daily walks came to a sudden stop. Pain had defeated me. A simple act of taking care of my needs became a monumental challenge. Sleep was not possible, and my ability to depend on myself was compromised.

Fortunately for me, this experience was temporary. At the present moment, I am totally healed and have rejoined my active life with gusto. The frightful experience has left me with a greater appreciation for what I had taken for granted. I really liked my old self, and I want to hang on to a sense of gratitude for my circumstances.

Applying what I learn in each instance leads to a new me, only wiser and stronger, ready to engage in the rest of the journey with a more positive attitude. Whether in an "aha" or a "hard learning" moment, I must open myself to receive the messages that lead me to new stages in the journey. If these messages become lessons learned, I have succeeded in reinventing myself.

Dysfunctional Childhoods

Many adults tend to think of their childhood as dysfunctional. I was one of them, until I realized our parents, like so many others, raised us for a future that never happened. I am even more cognizant of this fact in today's world, where technology has accelerated change that includes value systems, language, and behavior.

Enjoying the beach in Havana, 1942

There is indeed a disconnect between what we were taught as children and the world we eventually have to face. We can't confront the new environment without struggle, as the lessons passed to us do not seem to fit. My youngest brother was angry with our parents for not "preparing" him to meet his reality. Fortunately, he soon realized they were not "prepared" either and that it was his responsibility alone to figure out how to function in his life circumstances.

It is common for individuals to grow up with emotional scars from past experiences. Some feel parents favored one of their siblings. Others react to the discipline methods used at home. There are numerous other reasons people use as excuses to blame someone other than themselves for their failures. I strongly feel that dwelling on the negatives of our childhood and blaming others for any misery we may have experienced is unproductive, as most of the principals are no longer with us. We must find a way to get past this impulse, and it helps to think parents did the best they could, considering the challenges and limitations they encountered.

Analyzing our feelings helps us understand who we are and what the adjustments are that we must make to improve our chances of success. With this step achieved, we can freely move on with a lighter heart.

No Pain, No Gain

Aside from the fact that youth and the possibility of a longer future go together, there are few other things I miss from that stage in my life. Perhaps painless movement and better balance are two things I could be missing. But if I had a choice, I prefer the present. I would definitely not entertain living through the stress of being young all over again.

I spent my youth in search of self-confidence, of happier times, and of approval from others. Restricted by diets since age twelve, I sacrificed pleasurable experiences to look good for others. My subsequent years in the United States were not easy either. They were years of struggle— learning to cope with cultural differences, being a single mother with three jobs, and attending school with very limited financial resources. I missed the buoyancy of youth, and the best hope was for a future free of worry and anxiety. My youth was more a preparation for the future, and I was lucky I lived long enough to benefit from the sacrifice.

It was not until my forties that I could say I finally got my act together. The death of my son was a sudden awakening. I learned about surviving with half a heart, to question existence, and to find strength where I thought there was none left. My son motivated me to be, to be better, and to never give up. I learned to appreciate what I had left and to love a memory of whom he had been. I was able to pick up the pieces and live on, learn new things, and embark on new adventures.

I had been a lost soul in my thirties, and I was able to find myself in the face of grief. No longer in a hurry to get "nowhere," I now moved intentionally to ensure that every moment was lived with meaning.

Grief cannot be avoided, but we can appreciate the valuable lessons it provides. Even when, at first, Mother Grief has forgotten to provide the lesson, with time, we can uncover a valuable message. That happened to me when a twenty-three-year relationship ended in 2004. The breakup came as a shock at the time. I was unaware of any warning signs, except for a puzzling experience at our last New Year's celebration.

As the party was winding down, I noticed that my significant other was not joining in the festivities, choosing to stay in the kitchen, talking to friends who were staying with us through the holidays. As those guests were leaving, I noticed that one of them was crying while we hugged goodbye. I commented to my partner how strange that seemed, and she agreed.

To my surprise, two days after that incident, my partner announced that, since she had not been feeling well of late, she was going back to Houston to be checked by our physician. I thought that was prudent, so we prepared for her departure. At the time, I was holding a job of great responsibility, which did not allow me to accompany her. It was nothing serious, she assured me, and there was no need for me to go. I went about my life, checking to see how she was doing from a distance.

Suddenly the realization that she was not returning became all too clear, and for the first time, I knew this chapter of my life was over. I was consumed with rejection, stopped eating, and lost so much weight that I dropped from a healthy size 10 to an unhealthy 4. I could not think beyond my depression, my sense of failure, and the humiliation of being rebuffed. At times, I had to excuse myself from company and find a place to cry in private. I was at the bottom of a dark, cold, and lonely pit.

I had two choices—stay there and stop living or realize that "it takes two to tango" and look into what part I had played in this drama. In trying to reconstruct my shattered emotions, I was eager to find lessons to be learned. In retrospect, I realized I had not been entirely happy, but habit and loneliness had convinced me that the relationship was my destiny.

The fact that these events came as a surprise told me the whole story. Relationships do not survive silence or indifference. It takes work and dedication to fill an emptying cup, so it became clear that I had not carried my load. I did not know whether to be angry or hurt, so I chose both.

Taking a relationship for granted was not the way to feed it. I realized how little communication there had been through the years and how little of myself I had invested. As architect Jeff Daly once said, "Two monologues do not make a dialogue." I knew that listening and looking for silent signs were critical elements in establishing effective communication, but we had both failed to do that.

I came to the conclusion that the breakup could not be entirely one person's fault and that it would have helped to put the cards on the table from the beginning. Understanding that not being a good fit does not mean either partner is to be fully blamed allowed me to regain my peace of mind.

As time passed, I realized that breakups happen for a reason, and what better reason than being mismatched! It is healthy to let go of what is not for us and appreciate relationships that make us grow and enjoy life. When you stop sharing needs and dislikes with your partner, relationships collapse, a signal that those involved are growing apart.

Not Afraid to Fail

It is unfortunate that many people observe life through opaque lenses. These individuals tend to believe "no" is the appropriate response to most things in life. "This can't be done," "we'll never get there," and other versions of the negative are generally their first reactions. It is no wonder these individuals do not seem to expand their horizons beyond the narrow limits they set for themselves. Perhaps they fear failure more than they seek success. Those who do not conquer their fear of failure end up failing, preventing their dreams from becoming a reality.

When I was preparing to apply for a full professorship, I had to document a lifetime of accomplishments in teaching, service, and scholarly activities. My greatest concern was being turned down, being embarrassed and humiliated by failing to accomplish this important step in my career. Those feelings were almost insuperable obstacles to move up in my profession, and they almost won.

Celebrating the author's final retirement from Miami
Dade College, Kendall Campus, 2007

It was my friend and colleague Judy Márquez who alerted me to the risks of negativism. She helped me to see that, if I did nothing, I was actually bringing about failure. If I tried, at least there was a chance I could succeed. I took the chance, and my career moved forward. Fear was a form of paralysis, and I had pushed back past the gridlock it had caused. It worked.

The Fearsome Unknown

Human beings tend to fall into routines, their security blanket, intended to prevent surprises, one foot after the other—same old, same old. We don't realize that surprising events find their way into our lives without much fanfare. In such instances, we frequently become frightened, rather than motivated to leave behind our failed routines to try something new.

Those of us who chose exile were forced to survive the unknown by facing what lay beyond. We made space for new adventures. We found new homes, made new friends, learned new languages, and adapted to new forms of life. Most of us managed to survive and succeed by pushing ourselves beyond our comfort zones.

Others were not able to think past their fears, and chose their customary and time-honored existence. They may not have realized that circumstances do not stay put. Not only does time keep moving, it also takes you with it.

The issue becomes, who is in the driver's seat? Do you let life happen without much intervention on your part, or do you live intentionally, pushing yourself beyond fear and making something important to you happen? Conformism sometimes persuades some to believe that "*más vale malo por conocido que bueno por conocer*" (better the evil you know than the goodness you don't). But these individuals might be missing a worthwhile experience.

President Franklin D. Roosevelt, in his inaugural address, stated that the one thing we have to fear is fear itself, and I would add what a therapist once said to me. "When you get close to the cage, the monster you feared is not as menacing." I agree that when we move towards the cause of fear, we will find out it was not as frightful as it once seemed. Only then can we put that issue to rest and move forward.

Unfinished Business

Among my biggest concerns about the world of today are the effects of global warming. Right-wing politicians, putting party before country, have questioned and even denied its existence, but reputable scientists warn that we are polluting our planet, bringing about climate change.

The end of the world has been feared by many generations before mine, but for our grandchildren's peer group and beyond, it is a very real possibility. We can already see warning signs, in deadlier earthquakes, drastic weather changes, extraordinary floods, rapid ice melt, and other evidence suggesting that global warming is not a fairy tale.

There are considerable unanswered questions that all generations should be asking themselves, so together we can find the appropriate solutions. Is it too late for humankind to do something to reverse, or at least deter, the harmful effects of global warming? Is it too late to control the burning of fossil fuels, which exacerbate the warming of the atmosphere? Are the three R's—reduce, reuse, and recycle—enough to combat global warming? Are the inventions that have made our lives more comfortable the very tools that will bring about our end as a human-inhabited planet? Can some politicians or greedy industrialists realize our responsibility in accelerating our demise and develop policies that guarantee a future?

We worry about what to bequest our grandchildren. The best gift would be a clean earth with a future.

Another concern for what lies ahead is the threat to world peace. Terrorism and war endanger our ability to live in harmony, an essential ingredient for our survival. Death and destruction could never be an effective response to the world's troubles, just as suicide is not the solution to a hopeless life. To end something without finding a way out seems the same as burying one's head in the sand.

It is difficult to combat a terrorist who shows little or no respect for human life through schemes of irreparable damage.

I fear that we leave behind a world that is no longer safe, unless we all become involved in the fight to stop terrorism and deter global warming. I could not agree more with our Native American brothers and sisters in that, "We do not inherit the earth from our ancestors; we borrow it from our children."

Current Political Environment

On November 8, 2016, I felt our country was handed a death sentence. Donald Trump, a billionaire megalomaniac, was elected president of the United States. After losing by over two million votes to Hillary Clinton, the Electoral College, not the people, handed him the presidency. Cries of foul play, including the documented interference of Russia into our democracy, prompted Congress and the FBI to conduct a criminal investigation. These efforts were derailed by partisan politics.

My hopes for fairness and progress died on the day Trump, a man who had shown plenty of evidence of his unfitness to be commander in chief, was elected. For a while, I was not able to keep up with the news. I lived in fear of what I would find out. I talked to my children and shared my devastation. One was empathetic. She also felt my pain. We, as women, had fought mightily for the opportunity to shatter the glass ceiling and had missed the mark. I hope to have another chance to see a woman lead the most powerful country in the world before my moment arrives.

It took 240 years to elect the first African American President and to have the first female candidate for the presidency, but not without relentless and disproportionate scrutiny about every aspect of their lives. While some praised President Obama for rescuing the country from financial devastation, others blamed him for conditions he inherited. It is time for us Americans to ask ourselves, Was Obama the "worst president," as Trump has claimed, or the "first black president"? Is this really politics or deep-rooted racism? My answers are obvious, and it seems that the majority of the country agrees that Trump and most of his base are white nationalists who believe there is a superior race, theirs.

While candidate Clinton made history, it came at a price for her. Her detractors put her on trial with baseless allegations. Their "outrage" overlooked the value of her detailed policies and her extensive credentials. During the presidential campaign, Clinton was put on the defensive. Trump got a pass. He never shared his tax returns, a credible medical report, or clarifications of some questionable business practices. He made his way to the presidency without even showing contrition for his relentless racist and sexist name-calling.

Some thoughts continue to haunt me after his years in the presidency. Will we remain the "most powerful" force to guide the rest of the world toward democracy and social justice? Will we revert instead to old times, when the powerful were all white, all men? History takes its time to tell us, and I fear that, in the meantime, our progress will be stalled or even reversed. Our democracy is being tested.

After the first few months of the Trump presidency, we had already seen more involvement, more momentum from my fellow citizens to defend against the trampling of the Constitution. Women's marches all over the world have attracted millions of men, women, and children in support of equal rights for all. It has awakened those who were apathetic and has shown all of humanity that everyone has a part to play in this drama.

Although I do not want to make politics a major thrust of this book, a commentary regarding the current administration's pervasive attacks against immigrants is also necessary at this juncture. It is ironic that, in a country of immigrants, so much disdain and hatred can be sown against those fleeing their homeland, seeking liberty and hope. From erecting walls to separating families at the border, the climate against immigrants will make a future in this country an elusive, if not impossible, dream for many. I count my blessings that my family and I were able to take refuge in this land and become productive and free.

Reluctant to turn my life story into a political diatribe but compelled by the political circumstances of the moment, I must continue to digress so I can honor the fact that, three years into his presidency, Donald Trump has been impeached by the House of Representatives on the grounds of abuse of power and obstruction of Congress. The highly partisan nature of the Senate trial hid a mountain of evidence that supported Trump's impeachment and managed to use their majority power to vote against removing the president from office. Trump joins the fate of two other presidents who seemed to forget that no one is above the law. Time will ultimately judge his place in the annals of our history.

The world of today is closely interconnected, and whatever unfairness plays against one touches all of us. Becoming involved is no longer a choice. It is a responsibility that creates a path to a more inclusive future.

More Lessons Learned: Do's and Don'ts to Aging Gracefully

Mario Benedetti, the late Uruguayan journalist, novelist, and poet, once said, "In life, we must avoid three geometric figures—vicious circles, love triangles, and square minds." I could not agree more. During my life, I have identified some additional "guidelines" for a successful journey. I view them as a prescription to counterbalance the negativity associated with aging. Following is a list of potential therapies to support aging with joy.

1. Simplify, simplify.

We tend to complicate life by accumulating possessions or by getting lost in activities that serve more as escapes from reality than as conduits to happiness. I have learned that the simpler the life events, the greater the opportunity to enjoy every moment. Well-known German theologian Dorothea Solle said it best: "If my hands are fully occupied in holding onto something, I can neither give nor receive."

We complicate our existence with material possessions well beyond our needs. I hear of wealthy celebrities who own five or six mansions, and I often wonder if they can call any of them a home. Chinese philosopher Confucius warned us, "Life is really simple, but we insist on making it complicated."

Balance is the key to a peaceful journey, and too much is just as bad as too little. We must search for what is enough, so we can appreciate and enjoy what we have. Sometimes we are persuaded that we need things, only to find out in time that we never found a real use for them.

2. Stay optimistic and build positive memories.

"Be thankful for whatever you have; you'll end up having more. If you concentrate on what you don't have, you will never, ever have enough" (Actress Oprah Winfrey). Life is so much more pleasing when we approach it with optimism.

We should not fear failure; instead, seek the light at the end of the tunnel. It can be found if fear does not stand in our way. Having a can-do attitude helps us achieve our dreams and invite opportunities that enhance our lives.

We suggested earlier that life is like a necklace, a string of memories. If we build positive ones, they will lead us into a more meaningful and enjoyable journey.

3. Have no regrets.

Don't look back. Don't compare or think of *what might have been if* ... Have a bucket list and use it as a blueprint for new adventures to avoid regrets. If you desperately want something, don't postpone it; pursue it with passion.

As author E. A. Buchianeri advised, "Be wise today, so you don't cry tomorrow." Missed opportunities should be minimized at all cost, as they are a common cause of regret. I believe that making dreams into plans ensures their fulfillment.

Be cognizant that an incomplete dream becomes a regret.

4. Rely on humor to survive the journey.

Humor is a very effective vehicle to play down life's challenges. Laughter is the best medicine to conquer any threats to your peace of mind. It is common knowledge that humor reduces stress in our lives, and stress threatens our physical and emotional well-being.

Better the pain of laughing until our sides hurt than the one that comes from grief. American humorist Mark Twain went further: "Humor is the great thing, the saving thing, after all. The minute it crops, all our hardnesses yield, all our irritations, and resentments flit away, and a sunny spirit takes their place" ("What Paul Bourget Thinks of Us," 1918).

5. Don't blame others.

Assume responsibility for what happens and learn from your own mistakes, since you are in control of your actions.

Inspirational author Shannon Alder has stated, "People that have trust issues need to look in the mirror. There they will meet the one person that will betray them the most." It is incumbent upon us to look for lessons in life's events, as we hardly ever learn from the mistakes of others.

"It takes two to tango," so in any disagreement look for your responsibility in the matter. Finding out what part we played in any situation allows us to learn important lessons. Success tends to escape those who blame the world for their failures.

6. Live in the present.

Live the now. Make the best out of every moment and live it with delight, as if it were worthy of becoming a memory.

The past is gone, and now is your only opportunity to make tomorrow better. Sticking to the past will only prevent the future from happening. Accept that the past is no longer and that you are still around!

Skipping the now for the sake of a future event is a risky proposition, as the now is real and the future, uncertain. "Tomorrow is tomorrow. Future cares have future cures, and we must mind today" (Sophocles, *Antigone*).

7. Feed the adventurous spirit.

Honor your adventurous spirit, if you have been blessed with one. If not, welcome the opportunity to forge one.

Embrace the *new*. There is always some adventure or dream you can still pursue. Any opportunity to add *newness* to our lives should be encouraged, as boredom and fear keep people from moving forward in life.

Risk taking is a necessary step in enjoying new adventures. Without change, life is stagnant, and without risk taking, change does not happen. "Life is either a daring adventure, or nothing at all" (Helen Keller, *The Open Door*).

8. Consider life as borrowed time.

"We are travelers on a cosmic journey, stardust swirling and dancing in the eddies and whirlpools of infinity. Life is eternal. We have stopped for a moment to encounter each other, to meet, to love, to share. This is a precious moment. It is a little parenthesis in eternity" (new age author Deepak Chopra).

Love your friends and family, but consider them all as a temporary pleasure. Don't take them for granted, as they will not be around forever. Facing their loss will be harder if it is unexpected, but knowing that all of us are on borrowed time helps us derive pleasure from every moment of our lives together.

Stay strong in the face of loss of loved ones, but find comfort in their memories. Author Craig Loungsbrough agrees, "Death reminds us that life is a temporary privilege, not an endless right."

9. Embrace who you are.

"Accept yourself, your strengths, your weaknesses, your truths, and know what tools you have to fulfill your purpose" (Steve Maraboli, *Life, the Truth, and Being Free*). Stay real and, above all, be true to yourself.

Know that your best contribution to the world is becoming who you want to be. We all have one life to live, governed only by talent, capabilities, and limitations. Embrace your destiny. You don't get other choices.

And while you are at it, be proud of the signs of age. They are a testimony of your strength, not your weakness. Remember that youth and beauty are not what other people see but what you feel within you.

10. Stay in control of your destiny.

The late Hollywood comedian and dancer Danny Kaye felt that "life is a blank canvas, and you need to throw all the paint on it you can." We are in control of whether the paint creates a beautiful work of art or simply confusing globs of colors.

Life is your show. Decide for yourself and don't let anyone persuade you otherwise. One common misstep in not embracing the self is to allow others to take control of our lives, trying to change who we are. If all we do in life is give up important parts of our being for others without replenishing them, we devastate our life force in due course.

This is your parade. Do not let anyone rain on it.

===

At present, we are living through a world changing pandemic, Covid 19, that has taken many lives and threatens our very being. Most states in our country are enforcing security measures that have brought our lives to a halt.

In the midst of reexamining my values and choices, I realize that what is most at stake are changes within ourselves. Who will we be when a semblance of "normalcy" returns? I am concentrating on remaining strong and positive by undertaking activities that feed my spirit. I feel gratitude for what I have, for my family and friends, and for a fighting spirit that will not give up. If this is my end, I accept it. If it is not, I am working to become the person who lives every opportunity as a moment worth remembering.

Perhaps our next life, what some call heaven, is being young again with the wisdom we have garnered through the lessons life provides us as we continue our journey. We cannot tell others how to live, but we can certainly share what each of us has done in pursuit of a more gratifying journey.

EPILOGUE

The subtitle for this book, *An American Story of Survival*, was inspired by my mother's cooking. The "mother of invention," she learned the art in her sixties. If she lacked an ingredient, she would make do with what she had. Sometimes her creations were appetizing; others, not so much. But there was always a hot meal served. That message can be translated into our daily lives. Do what you can with what you have, and life will happen. I hope to continue being guided by my mantra, "It is what it is," to be more accepting of my reality, and to move on with intention.

I have shared with you the story of my life, low ebbs and high points, just like everyone else's journey. I have also described resources I have used to enhance the quality of my time on this earth with the purpose of inspiring others to not only survive but also thrive. I have learned three significant lessons in the art of survival—(a) looking for meaning in my actions and interactions, (b) embracing the moment, and (c) ensuring the absence of regrets. I particularly value the audacity of not giving in when challenges disrupted my journey. Moving past those encounters allowed me a life without resentment and a sunnier outlook shaped by gratitude.

Being intentional in what we do or say promotes meaningful outcomes in decisions we make. It is satisfying to follow a plan with positive impact on your life or on the lives of others. Although intentionality requires planning, it does not prevent us from enjoying the moment. As American philosopher-physician Debasish Mridha reminds us, "Life is happening at this very moment; it is not behind us or before us. The past is full of memories, and the future is full of expectations." (*Verses of Happiness*). It is obvious that we must embrace the now; any action that can change our world can only happen in the present moment.

I hope to have communicated a most important lesson taught by my ageless father. He strongly believed that there was a difference between getting older and being old. To him, the secret was attitude, rather than actual age. That belief allowed him, in his nineties, to dance the jig at the Irish wedding of one of his grandnephews, despite the fact that rhythm was not one of his gifts.

In my dad's mind, an old person stopped dreaming and favored living in the past, while the forever young in spirit looked at aging with acceptance, as a process that "was what it was." Being able to live in the present without disrupting dreams of our uncertain future was his secret weapon to age gracefully and with the hope that those dreams will become.

While in the process of writing this book, I received the news that Fidel Castro had passed away. After so many years of pent-up anger, my mind was blank at the news. My heart, however, sang a different tune. It was the tune of hope—hope for Cubans still living on the island that they may gain their freedoms, hope that regimes that shatter dreams and kill the spirit will no longer be, hope that someday the sacrifice of giving up our homeland will allow our next generations to pursue the American dream. Days later, I wrote the following piece for our local newspaper, *The Santa Fe New Mexican:*

After Castro, a Ray of Hope for Freedom

On November 25, 2016, at 10:29 p.m. eastern standard time, the longest ruling despot died. Fidel Castro Ruz is gone, but his legacy of death and destruction lives on. He leaves behind a broken people, a result of his failed experiment in Cuba. Although retiring from the presidency due to ill health in 2006, his Marxist-Leninist philosophy has remained in power for 57 years. Perhaps for the impoverished Cubans still living on the island, not much will change, but for the exile community, a sense of relief and liberation serve as temporary solace for a lost homeland.

Some people have been critical of the joy expressed in the streets of Little Havana, in Miami, celebrating a death, but Castro's demise is not an ordinary event. He robbed exiles of their homeland, their families, their friends, their belongings. Although the streets were bustling with music, dance, and other expressions of joy, exiles are really in mourning.

We grieve for those no longer here to share in the news, the ray of hope that Cuba will be free someday. I think of my parents, who in their sixties had to start life anew, having lost everything. I think of my caretaker Tata, who was with me from the time I was seven days old until I left Cuba at nineteen. I never saw her again. I think of my late brothers, who would have rejoiced with the expectation of a free Cuba. I think of my friend Alberto, who died in Bay of Pigs like so many who dared fight against oppression. I think of another friend, Mayito, who spent twenty years in prison for being somebody's nephew. I think of so many others, the *balseros*, who lost their lives trying to escape the island in homemade vessels.

My friends want to know how I feel. The monster, our tsunami, is dead.